Freedom from the Trick Bag

FREEDOM *from the* TRICK BAG

TESHAWN LOGAN

HARRIS
Author Services
worldwide

DEDICATION

This book is first dedicated to God. You put it in my heart ten-plus years ago. Who knew after all these years that you were waiting for me to fully surrender my life to get this book started so every area in which I struggled I would be totally surrendered to You? I give You all the honor, glory, and praise for You alone are my Father.To my co-author, Mr. Facebook! You are my king, and the head of my house. You have been encouraging throughout all of my endeavors, and I praise God that you listened to my directions from God. You are a hard-working man, and if we had not done things God's way, this book would not have been possible. Thanks for all your strong words of encouragement, your motivation to be more like Jesus, and your effort as the head of my house. Thanks for helping me complete the missing puzzle to this book (you); without you this book would not exist. Most important, thanks for your faith because it has moved many mountains throughout all our ups and downs!

To Cerina! I thank you for motivating me when you were born and throughout your childhood to climb out of the trick bag. In return, you helped me to change my evil ways and helped me become the *godly mom, mentor, and prayer warrior I am today. You have a great head on your shoulders. Hopefully, this book will save you a trip from the trick bag.*

To Camari, Aj, Justice, and Taeya! May you stand firm and bold on the word of God even if you have to stand alone, and no matter how handsome or beautiful you have become, always remember that character counts when no one else is watching, and character is what you will take to Heaven.

To Aunt Saundra! Thank you for helping me transition out of alcoholism. You always said that it is not going to be easy giving up self, but it will be worth it, and I always held true to those words and stand here today to say it's definitely worth the peace of mind.

To my true mentor, prayer warrior, and good friend Pastor George Williams! Thanks for always, and I mean always picking my phone calls up and allowing me to ask questions. When I was at my lowest, you prayed for me and spoke a word over me, which made a huge difference, and I'm here to speak about it today. If it weren't for you and Sister Williams praying over my life, I would still be in bondage to porn today. Lastly, if it weren't for that 5 a.m. prayer line, I would have never gotten such clear directions and guidance about my soon-to-be husband. You told us to tell our story, and here we are telling it to the world.

To Pastor Pierre Quinn! Thank you for your

guidance and endless prayers and for always being positive no matter what the circumstances are.

To my girls, Faith, Nikki, Rhonda, and Kenyatta! Thank you for encouraging me to be a better woman of God and always having my back.

To my parents! Thank you for being patient throughout all these years and praying for my salvation. I know it was all your prayers that kept me even when I wasn't in my right mind. I do not regret one thing, but I know for sure that you will reap what you sow.

CONTENTS

INTRODUCTION OF THE TRICK BAG

The trick bag is anything that keeps you in bondage. Let's be clear. I'm not here to judge, talk about the different candies that were in the bag, or point the finger at you. I'm simply talking about me and some of the things that happened in my life that I did not allow to hold me down. This book reveals the most transparent part of my journey so that others may be set free. Do not get it twisted, I was the trick, but I'm here to remind you that Jesus hung with and healed the tricks. So you know He healed this trick so I can come back and show you that no matter what, "It works!"

What you do in the trials molds you into who you are today. Be prepared to be delivered!

THE
BACKSTORY

My husband and I agreed that for my testimony to boldly reveal the power of God to change a wretch like me, I needed to be transparent and share the whole ugly truth. My ego was embarrassed to reveal just how degraded I had become. What I'm most embarrassed about is that I crucified the Son of God once again and openly shamed Him. I didn't want people to judge me by my past, but the more I thought about Jesus risking His all to save me, I thought I would do the same to help give even one person hope whom Jesus can save from the "gutter most to the uttermost!" My story simply shows how dark and low we will sink when we are halfhearted and our feet remain planted one in the church and the other on the broad way to destruction. Satan exalts! For you think you are on God's side when in reality he is your master. Christ said no man can serve two masters (Matthew 6:24).

Many have a form of godliness but deny His power to keep them from this degenerate age and its vices, better known as the trick bag. Freedom can be yours today!

Turn around today! The devil lies and whispers that you've gone too far. No, you haven't! At least, not yet. There will come a time when He will say, "It is finished. He that is unjust let him be unjust still. He that is filthy, let him be filthy still" (Revelation 22:11).

Maybe you already have plans that you know will cause you to be unfaithful to God today. Don't worry; there is hope!

Even if the room has been paid for, you have the hotel key in your hand, and your ex (really evil spirits) is waiting in the hotel room, it is not too late to make a different decision. Only a look to Jesus will give you the strength and courage to love Him more than you do yourself, to want to please Him and be faithful to Him.

Revelation 7 gives a picture of four angels holding back the trouble and strife about to break forth on this earth, but why are they holding back? They wait till God numbers His people and forever seals them in righteousness.

Doesn't that make you joyous? God loves us so much that He says, "Wait a minute, hold up! Not yet. I'm looking at the clock, and I know it's past time to wrap this thing up. But you do not have My permission to let go the four winds of strife just yet. You see, I'm working with somebody. My girl, Teshawn, is about to get this thing together. Let's hold off for just another minute until I have sealed this girl and all of my other children in their foreheads!" Come on, now. How can that not be a cause for a shout; can I get an Amen?

You can have the same forgiveness, joy, and peace He has given me. This is why I tell my uncut story; get ready for change.

1

#METOO

Often we do not recognize why we do the things we do until we revisit our past. This defines habits and reasons for why we do what we do. We act out behaviors that should not be a part of our makeup, and we end up being tormented and bitter. Why? It all derives from the root. Who would have thought that I would have experienced a "Me Too" moment at such a young age? My thinking was that out of everyone in the entire world, families are the people whom we are supposed to trust. Unbeknownst to Grandma, everything was happening right behind her back—more like in front of her face, but she wasn't aware.

Let's get something straight: I grew up in a household with one older brother, and we did not just do what we pleased like other kids we knew. We did not eat unhealthy foods, which would explain my brother's and my perfect teeth at the time, or go wherever we felt like going. We had a wonderful childhood and came from a very structured home. We both were brought up learning about God, His commandments, and His diet, and at a very young age I learned about many scriptures that carried me through my tough times later on in life. What do you do when your mom does the best she can to protect you and give you everything you need to be a child, and you still end up being taken advantage of? My brother and I could not go to anybody's house. Mom did her best to make sure we were sent with family members who would honor our way of living and maybe a close friend or two of hers whom she knew would be super-loyal to her standards, and trust me, these people amount to a limited few.

Honestly, one of the main houses she trusted us to go to was the main house I hated going to. It was grandma's house because she made it very clear we had to stay in her yard and not run off to anyone else's house in the neighborhood. That was very hard to do because it was like God telling Adam not to eat from the specific tree in the Garden of Eden that was so tempting because He said, "Do not eat" from that tree. There was nothing to do but run outside and play with sticks or run up and down her long dirt road and maybe see a few cousins every now and then. Other than that, there was nowhere to go unless she decided to take us to the water, which was the next road over, and then was the biggest thing of all: I had to see the same person who I had no idea at the time was taking advantage of me. Even though I hated going to grandma's, I somehow got used to liking what was going on whenever we had to go over there; mind you I was eight or nine years old at the time.

I can't remember all the details because it was so long ago, but I can remember it was different, especially when most people thought that males were the ones who take advantage of little kids. Nope, not this time. This was a female. I later started acting these same behaviors out when I spent the night at various girlfriends' houses, even though I did not think it was wrong, and I'm pretty sure the other females did not think anything of it; we were young. I figured, this is what friends do, right? I had this crazy upper body fetish and had no idea why for a very long time.

Ladies, this is why it is essential to cover your breast cleavage and butts when you are out and about, especially at church. We have got to get to a higher place in life so we are not known as thirsty, but rather classy; be original. By the way, my definition of thirsty means wanting to attract the wrong kind of attention whether you are married or single. Understand there are men and women out there who have overcome different fetishes such as boobs, arms, butts, legs, thighs, and feet, and every time they see you uncovered or showing too much flesh, it puts them back in the same mindset of that which was supposed to be overcome. I make it very clear to all of my relatives, friends, and so on that if they come over my house, they make sure they do not have too much showing because I do not want to be reminded of what I overcame.

I remember hearing a sermon by one of my favorite pastors, who said, "However you dress reflects your relationship with God," and from that point on I was mindful of how I dressed. I hate to even bring up this point, but I can't neglect the fact that I did not have boobs until the end of my ninth-grade year going into tenth. The simple fact is that whenever I got around that person, those were the only thoughts I had because she always wanted me to touch her boobs. Always remember that hurt people hurt people, and most of the time, it is not their fault because someone most likely abused them, so they are acting out what happened to them. Or perhaps nothing happened; it is just this crazy word that we forget about called sin.

Growing up I had a free lifestyle. We did not watch a lot of television or play video games; rather we spent our days, especially after school outside in nature, playing with the Brown boys. Now, that is country for you. We had a big backyard, and our yard mixed with the next-door neighbor's yard. We hiked through the woods, built tree houses, had a dog to play with until he died and was replaced with another, and played hide and go seek, kickball, football, basketball, and baseball. You name it, and we did it. Although I had a great childhood, I can't ignore the fact that in my later childhood years, like, eleven or twelve, I was being nosey and got exposed to someone's porn collection, which we will discuss shortly.

Growing up, my brother was three years older than I. He was a ladies' man. He was handsome, could sing, and was outgoing. A lot of guys hated him because of his talents, and did I forget to highlight he was gorgeous? My brother liked women, and women loved him. It is like they would throw themselves at him. I would even go as far as to say that a family member liked him; yes, he was that cute. My brain should be forever scarred by having an older brother, but only by God's grace and mercy, He has given me the victory over every ungodly thing I have ever seen.

I always thought of myself as a tomboy. I fought boys; I had no chest. I was the only girl in the neighborhood and had no other females to hang with except the neighbors on the other side of us, but that is another story. I dressed like a boy, and one day I tried to pee like a boy. I got teased because I had no chest, as some would say flat-chested, and I even had a mustache that I was embarrassed about. I will admit I liked hanging around my brother and his friends during the times my brother and I were not at each other's throats. This is because they always had something to do like riding dirt bikes, motorcycles, and go-carts, going to this place called the pit and riding four-wheelers. Do you get it?

The only part I hated was when they would make plans to go see the girls. I was very protective of my brother, and I'm sure it showed. I had to be his pit bull by fighting off these girls, and trust me, that was a waste of time because he was a man, so although a sweetheart, he would naturally do what men do: play games. I was not wasting my time going to see those girls; my mom probably would not let me go with the boys anyhow. Actually, my parents, for the most part, would not let him go anywhere unless I were with him. I looked up to my older brother; we had a great childhood together. We had typical sibling quarrels, but he was definitely my protector, as older brothers are. He never wanted me to hang with his friends because he did not want his friends to try to get with me or me to like them. How about this? He did not want me in any boy's face. We really had a genuine love for each other.

The porn habit all started when I used to sneak over to a family member's house. This is where I was exposed to Jerry Springer uncut, and there I came across someone's porn collection, which caused me to be super inquisitive about what this sex thing was all about. It did not happen right away; it was gradual. From then on I was hooked on the wrong things and could not wait to watch more. Shortly afterward, because I wasn't sexually active, I had to release these feelings. As most preteens do, I started abusing myself. I'm not even sure how I knew how to do that. Maybe I learned from the fast girls at school. I am not sure, but I do know that nobody taught me. Again, maybe it was sin because we were all born in sin and shaped in iniquity (Psalms 51:5).

The crazy part is that nobody knew that I was feeling or experiencing any of this. I did not tell my parents, and as tight as my brother and I were, I never told him. All these thoughts and emotions were locked away in my secret place, my mind. I was the sweet typical country girl, too curious, and I always like hanging with older people, and I always had a plan B. I never liked my age, so why should I like the people in my age group? I felt like kids my age could not give me any lessons on anything; they still had milk behind their ears; they were boring! I felt because I hung around older people that they could shed some light on life, and I would be there to take it all in like a sponge. I always thought I was older, and even now I still have older friends—I mean, like, over fifty. Looking back I never thought that coming across that collection of porn would lead me into another era of serious bondage.

How did I get to my smoking era? When I was younger, my next-door neighbor and I used to act as though we were smoking by rolling up grass in some type of huge leaf and finding some type of match to light it up. That is some typical country stuff. By eighth grade I was introduced to the real deal, smoking Black & Milds. Guess how? Hanging with my brother and his friends, which gave no high, but I thought I was cool. It was definitely popular, and everyone was doing it, and because I just knew that I knew what I was doing, I already had practiced with the leaves, remember? I was young and dumb.

I remember my brother saying the first time, "If you inhale and cough, that is it. You won't catch me giving you any more." So, of course, I had to fake the funk and inhale without coughing so I could be cool in my brother's eyes. After all, when you are young and dumb, you do dumb things, right? In 1998, toward the end of my ninth-grade year, the most overwhelming tragedy happened to me. My brother was killed in a car accident on Mother's Day. After this, my life totally changed for the worse. I remember so clearly. I went away for that weekend to sing with my school's choir at Pine Forge Academy for some Friday night service, stayed at my good friend's house that Saturday night because she lived close to the high school I was attending, and caught a ride to school in the morning to catch the bus to go to Kings Dominion that Sunday morning. I remember being at Kings Dominion and feeling in my gut that something bad had happened, but I could not understand my feelings.

I told myself, Watch, when I get home, I'm going to hear some bad news. First off, we were on a school field trip, and everyone on that trip was acting very nice to me. Whatever I wanted, they gave it to me; it could be anything from ice cream to pizza to a glass of water. It was almost as if they did not want me to ask questions about anything while on the trip. Everyone was working together to hold back the bad news because most of the high school class on the trip already knew what the bad news was. It was escalating around me at the amusement park, and I had no idea.

Finally, the bus arrived at my school only, I found my aunt and uncle instead of my parents were picking me up. I thought, Hmmm that is odd; where are my parents?

The entire ride home for an hour and something away, my aunt and uncle seemed to talk me to death to keep me from asking them any type of questions. Then there was silence. I could remember my aunt's bloodshot eyes and my asking her why her eyes were so red; she said, "It is my allergies," and believe you me, I was not going to fight her on that considering that it seemed my family members always had some type of allergy.

I thought, Let me fall asleep so they can stop talking me to death. We finally arrived at my house at the time, which was a cute little trailer with minimal space in the front yard. It managed to fit at least fifteen cars that night. I did not question the cars because we always had gatherings because of my large family. I walked up the stairs, and someone came out the door to stop me from entering my house, and then my mom slipped out to greet me. I look at my mom, and her face and eyes seemed blood-flushed from what I could remember. I remember her holding me real tight and saying, "You know I love you right?"

I'm thinking to myself, Oh shoot, am I in trouble? Did someone tell on me for kissing some boy? Although I thought I was a tomboy, I was a fresh tomboy. All these thoughts were running through my mind. I remember asking one question, "Where is Jr.'s car?" Then it hit me like a ton of bricks with a skyscraper on top and a weight tied to it that sunk at the bottom of the ocean.

Mom quietly shared the story of that morning at 8:30 or 9, Jr. and another young man who was in the car with him were on their way back from the laundromat. The other young man was in the hospital in critical condition, and somehow I did not manage to hear anything else but that Jr. lost control of the car because his axel broke. He ran into a tree and died immediately. If he had lived he would have been a vegetable. My whole world shut down; my heart seemed to race with anxiety, and in that instance, the world seemed to stop for that one minute after I heard, "Your brother died."

This means he will never come home; we will never eat dinner together, laugh again, vent about my parents, share the same room again, and make happy memories again. We will never go to church again, hug again, and speak again. I will never be an aunt or have a niece or nephew, I thought. And then to hear that the other guy was in the hospital? I immediately remembered with utter disbelief and looking up and seeing a clear sky with a million stars in it and yelling, "No!" as if that loud cry would bring him back or let me see him one more time.

Let me tell you why I yelled no. Remember, I told you about the friend's house I stayed at the night before the trip to Kings Dominion? Well, she and my brother used to date, and he was talking to her on the phone. Before they ended the call, my brother and I had a fallout for some dumb reason I can't remember. I remember him asking her to speak to me and tell me that he loved me, and I never said I love you back because in my mind I thought I would tell him the next day. Well, tomorrow never came because that tomorrow was when he died.

Some of you are harboring foolishness with a friend, family member, coworker, or parent because of money, embarrassment, shame, or guilt. What happens when tomorrow never comes, and something happens to that person that makes you feel trapped like a caged bird for a very long time? You have to ask yourself, "Is it really worth being miserable for the rest of your life?"

I often say if I could have only said, "I love you," or if I did not fight him as much or spent more time uplifting him instead of beating him down, what could I have done differently? Do not harbor these things. When you have an altercation with someone, get it straight immediately. Ephesians 4:26 says: "Be ye angry, and sin not: let not the sun go down upon your wrath." How many of us would be free? Do you want to experience freedom, or do you want to wallow in bitterness? What a terrible place to be when things aren't right in the family.

The next day I went to school because I could not handle seeing my parents cry all day for a straight week. They cried so hard and so much their eyes were bloodshot. I'm a happy person, and because I'm happy, I did not want to be around sadness. Well, the truth of the matter is I thought I could handle going to school, but it was worse. The entire ride to school I cried.

One of my older friends, who was like a sister to me, picked me up from school, and I stayed at her house for three weeks to get myself together. The church my brother attended wanted to have a candlelight service remembering him on one of those nights, and it was pretty sweet. I must admit that I cried through it, and I may have said some brief words, but I do not remember. My older cousin, who is like my older brother, sat beside me and consoled me the entire service. It was so sad.

I think it was sad because my brother touched many lives. After his nonsense years and almost becoming a young man, he was a powerful influence. He was the leader of his pack; he kept all these guys who had no real manly influence together. It seemed everywhere his presence was known; he touched people, from the drug dealers to the fatherless, to women, to older women, and to children. Prior to his funeral we were able to view the body; this really helped us cope during the funeral.

My brother's funeral was a blessing. This put things into perspective as the scripture says: what the enemy meant for evil, God will turn it around for good (Genesis 50:20). Three different schools or more were shut down because my brother touched so many lives. It seemed like every church in the Adventist conference also attended his funeral. One school came all the way from Pennsylvania; there were a few busloads there. I remember singing with the Pisgah Church's youth choir, "You Don't Have to Worry," by Kirk Franklin. I can't believe I had the strength to stand up there and sing. Then a girl he was crushing on at one point signed a powerful song, "The Battle Is Not Yours," by Yolanda Adams, and afterward she fell apart.

After the pastor finished preaching, he asked my mom to say a prayer, and I forgot to mention my mom is one of the most powerful prayer warriors I knew at the time. It was like when she stood in that pulpit, the heavens opened and the sun shined on her giving her extra power for that day to endure burying her son. The best part about the funeral was out of 2,000-odd people who attended, a hundred of them gave their lives to Jesus Christ! Now, that is a big deal. After all, Jesus Christ and all of Heaven rejoice over one soul, so that day was huge in Heaven. This is hope.

Shortly after my brother died I started acting out and did not know how to handle my emotions. My brother had such a powerful leash on me that after he passed away I went crazy. I ended up changing from my private school to the public school he attended and lost my innocence hanging with the wrong group of raunchy girls. I wanted to experience the limelight like them, only to find out it wasn't worth it. I mean I literally gave it away to some knucklehead who did not deserve my goodness just to see what I was missing, and I stand here to say it was not a blankety-blank thing.

The very next day the guy I had sex with went to school and told the whole school about our little rendezvous, which was supposed to be special and private. I was so embarrassed because my brother just died, and I was popular—the new kid on the block, if you want to call it that.

The next year I started sneaking out of my parents' house for months because I met a guy in school who I thought I was in love with, and I found it interesting because I got a taste of that forbidden sexual fruit. The first guy was some garbage, but that second guy, geesh, I really thought he cared about me and loved me. Like little Mo said in one of her songs, "It was the sex that was blinding me."

He was two years older than I, and we went to the same school; you know how it is when you date your first crush. He was the first person to teach me how to drive a stick shift. He also let me drive on various back roads to get experience behind the wheel. His parents adored me. I had

a great relationship with his sisters, and we had great conversations. I was in love (really lust), and I had it set in my
mind that when I graduated, I was going to marry him.

By the eleventh grade, I got put back in private school. I'm
sure it was due to my mom's wanting me to leave the love
of my life alone. That did not stop a thing. I was skipping
school to meet up with him at every opportunity I got. I was
also going down to the clinic to make sure I wasn't pregnant. This was a hot mess. Halfway through my junior year,
I thought it was cute to skip school, so I started shopping
with various girlfriends or run their errands, or just give
them company until they met up with their dudes.

One day I decided to skip school to catch the train with one
of my girls to go to her boyfriend's house in Southeast. I
do not know why I went with her because I knew this guy
was beating her. How could she think this dude loved her
when he was beating the crap out of her? She would come
to school with a black eye, and I never understood how
someone's love for a significant other could run so deeply
that they would be willing to risk being abused for that person. I was trying to be a loyal friend.

On this particular day, they got into it, and you would not
believe what happened. He beat her, and here I was. My
tomboy ways kicked in so I was trying to play the big guy
and save her, and his butt smacked me in my face. That
was my first and last time going over to his house with her.
The nerve of him! I had never been hit by a dude up to this
point, and I wasn't going to start. I'm just glad the smack

mark disappeared by the time I got home. I could not even tell my parents. If I did, I would be snitching on myself for skipping school.

Eventually, I and the fake love of my life broke up. He ended up cheating on me when he went away to college. I guess my mom had too many rules for him to follow. Come on, I was younger than him anyhow. Thinking back, I see there is no way a worldly man was going to go away to college and wait for someone in the eleventh grade. Now that I'm older I can see both sides. It did not make sense to think that the dude was going to save himself from all the other 500 girls just for me. College is twenty women to one man.

One evening on my way to a junior-senior banquet at school, I was silently introduced to drinking by someone who I thought at the time was a friend and whom my mom totally trusted. I'm thinking she liked anyone besides my boyfriend at the time, and maybe because this guy shared our religious background she felt comfortable, but the very next year I ended up pregnant by the same person she trusted because of drinking.

My first drink was a Wild Irish Rose. This was the strongest drink I had ever consumed and because of my addictive personality and my family history of alcoholism, I never knew that taking that one drink would later cause me to be a third-generation alcoholic. Although the addiction to alcohol skipped my mom, it seemed to take a deep dive into me. If only I had known that my grandfather had an alcohol addiction, my lips would have never touched the tip of that bottle. I must admit it felt really good being lost in my misery. It was exciting and fun and I got into the most trouble when I was drunk. Alcohol was to blame, and I could care less. It was exciting, and at that time I was all about doing me. I was not thinking of my parents and the fact that they had lost a son a just few years prior. I tell you, we can really be selfish sometimes, can't we?

I was sixteen starting my senior year in high school and was all about having fun, until I went away to check out a college that I had no intentions of going to. My dad thought I needed to clear my head and experience the hype of this college, my mom did not think I was ready. My dad convinced her to let me go see what it was like to go away for school. I mean, come on. I was a senior, my last year in school, about to be an adult. I'm trying to paint the picture.

Prior to my leaving, I remember mom calling the principal on the phone, and maybe the teachers, and did everything in her strength to ensure I had the proper supervision while on that trip. The principal assured her that I would have the proper supervision and that I would be in good hands. Guess what? When I arrived not only did I have freedom, I stayed in a dorm that had no curfew, let alone supervision. I was on cloud 1320. My parents had no idea that I was a free bird spreading my wings once again in a country setting, a foreign land, and there I was reintroduced to drinking by the same person.

I remember bumping into him and feeling super comfortable because I did not know anyone on the tour. I was ten states away from home and felt like he was my homeboy. He took me to a secluded place, and there I trusted him, so I talked and talked and talked about past situations and relationships. Then he knew how to work his plans of showing me a good time while on the tour. Guess what he asked me. Did I want to have fun? You know it, and that night I was doing just that. Lord, forgive me; I was on that campus having fun.

He came to pick me up at the unsupervised dorm, and he had some Wild Irish Rose. I bought a pack of Black and Milds while on the road, so I was good to go. I mean, hey, he knew the spots to go to, people to meet, places to hang, and most important, he was older than I. Remember, this put me in the mindset of being cool. It was something similar to how I felt about my brother, someone I looked up to.

The next day in the midst of our working our plans, I asked Mom if I could visit my god sister. I remember her telling me not to leave because my sister lived off-campus, but what did I do? You know what I did, what was expected from a rebellious sixteen-year-old. I defied her and thought nothing of it. Mind you, I was a great liar, or so I thought; plus she was over eighteen hours away from me, and you really think I was going to listen to my mom?

I was about to be grown up. My birthday was a few days away. Please. I wanted to visit my god sister. I wanted freedom and independence, and I wanted fun. That was the plan, and the guy and I were supposed to hook up and finish what we started from the night before. My only dilemma was getting back to the campus on time, which was the farthest thing from my mind. I do not know how I got to my god sister's house, but I know when I arrived I had the perfect meal. It was almost like it could have been my last meal, it was so good.

The guy ended up picking me up from my sister's house; we went to do our thing until, boom, we got caught up and ended up getting busted on our way back onto the campus, it was the very thing all of us on the tour feared, getting busted. Then those words from my mom's mouth came to bite me in my cheeks like a viper, "Be sure your sins will find you out" (Numbers 32:23). How on earth did we get busted? I will sadly tell you. My curfew bracelet snuck out from my sleeves and then those fearful words came from the window as we made our way back on campus thinking that everything was all good.

I may be exaggerating a bit because that was eighteen years ago, and I was a little tipsy, but it went something like this. Someone asked the driver, "Have you been drinking, or are you drunk?" From that point on, we could not enter the campus because we were drunk. The next thing you know cops were questioning us. I'm lying; he's snitching and playing the blame game, then I did it. I was always taught by my brother that the code was to never snitch, and I was a good liar back then. So, I told a lot of lies, and I even tried to lie my way out when we got stopped for breaking curfew and to finagle my way out of this one but nope, not this time. I was a lobster in boiling water. I had to tell the cops or whoever was interrogating me that we just came from having sex and it was possible that I could be pregnant. Of course, I was just frustrated and saying that because he snitched and told mostly everything. See, he was in boiling water because I was sixteen and he was twenty. I also believe the cops were threatening to lock him up, and in some states they will lock you all the way up to rot, especially in some racist states.

This was the second-most devastating situation to happen to me. Why? I not only had to write a statement but I had to call home to tell my mom what happened and that it was possible that I could be pregnant. Now, who would have really thought that one or two times having sex could get you pregnant? I was mad because I did not know what he told them, but when those people came back to interrogate me, they were like, "What happened? And this time we want the truth," so I decided to go all-in. Well, little did I know I would end up getting pregnant in another state. I was vulnerable. I trusted him, and he promised me that I would not get pregnant before we started.

Meanwhile, the entire college found out about my curfew ordeal. Not only was I humiliated, but I was angry because I was about to get in trouble. Then I had to run over and over in my head that I might have to face the consequences of possibly being a mother at an early age. I had to face my parents, but most important, I had disappointed God, the One I forgot about as I was having my so-called fun. Shortly after finding out I was pregnant, I ended up leaving my private school and going back to the public school to save face. I had to take counseling so the private school could have the situation documented due to their trying to make it seem as though I were crazy. It was just humiliating.

I was very sad during my pregnancy because I was young. It was my last year in high school, and I was supposed to be going to college. Although I heard of guys not wanting to claim a child they helped produce, I never thought I would experience another "Me Too" moment. Carrying this child, I became very sad because, let's keep it 100 percent true, this dude and I were not together. There was definitely an attraction; we were so-called friends, and in my mind I wondered how someone who was supposed to be my friend could treat me like that.

Back then, when you were pregnant in high school, they would send you to another school, so you could get the proper care needed during school hours and not miss out on schoolwork. At this school there was an awesome community of support for the girls who were expecting, and at this school we built bonds with each other. Some girls had their babies a few months before I did, and some did after. I met someone who became a very good friend. Not only did she look out for me, but also her family took us on. At the end of the day, we looked out for each other. It was a very nice support system that she and I had.

I'm very grateful I went to this school because I do not think I would have survived in a regular school. I was always tired, irritated, sad, and hungry, and at this school they allowed us to eat and sleep during school hours. I'm thankful I survived until graduation, and at nine months pregnant I walked across the stage with my daughter. Seven months into my pregnancy one of my friends introduced me to a guy who was my age. This guy really stepped in and helped me for the remainder of my pregnancy, and a few years after, we were engaged, but it did not last. After graduating from high school, I always thought education was the move for me, and since I did not go away to college, I attended the community college not too far from my house for a year or so.

Within that same year, I moved out of my parents' house to raise my daughter, and because I wanted to make my own choices and come and go as I pleased, I figured I had made my bed hard, so I had to do what I had to do. Now that I had moved out, I felt like a free bird. I was a woman! The sky was the limit. I obtained my first townhouse through the state and had to pay according to my income, but I did not care because it was something I could say was mine. I had a two-bedroom, one-bath townhouse and was living life, if you asked me.

During college, I met a man whom I could not stand at first. I thought he was annoying, but low and behold he ended up being a serious lover. I was in crazy bondage with this dude for nine years. I'm not saying moving out on my own was a bad thing, but I tell you when I did that this cocky guy I could not stand came over, and the next thing I knew I was so sexually connected with this dude, it was ridiculous. You ever had a dude call you at 3 a.m. for a booty call and command you through the phone to be up when he arrived?

He was the type of dude who put it down so good that you could not wait for him to get there.

Have you ever been in a situation where it took that person an hour to get to you and as tired as you were when they arrived, all of a sudden it seemed as though a Mountain Dew energy drink hit you in the head? I mean, these men had the nerve, especially when I had two jobs and had to be to work at a certain time, leaving me to sleep for two hours. But guess what? I always made room for action because I knew what was about to go down; plus, you could not tell me he wasn't the one for me. Just being in this person's presence made me feel alive, and yes, that was some good dopamine!

Remember the fiancé I mentioned earlier? Well, he was the one who talked me out of marrying the guy. What a sad case I was, listening to another man. Then to make it worse, when things did not work out with the other dudes, guess who was in the picture? He was a boyfriend at one point, but then he graduated to later becoming something I liked to call "my piece," by which I mean his penis was mine, and I definitely put tabs on him because he was putting it all the way down on me, and my mind was gone. Not to give this guy credit, but this guy messed my head up so much so that he made it difficult for everyone I dealt with. I mean, every guy I dated after that was never good enough because I was in so much bondage with this guy and really felt he loved me and had my best interest at heart. I think this was my first real experience tampering with the lust demon.

Listen, our relationship wasn't always sexual. We had a very good friendship. Not only was he outgoing, but I could also talk to him about anything, and we never got mad at each other. I mean, how can you really get mad at someone who was putting it down like that? I was beyond satisfied. At one point he became my best friend, and I can't even mark which point that was because there were so many interactions with him.

It all started when we got assigned to complete a task in college. He came to my house, met my mom, and thought my mom would love his mom because they are cut from the same cloth, meaning they loved the Lord and were very spiritual. Guess what? He never lied about that. So he introduced his mom to mine, and they became very good friends. Then his mom really blessed me because she used to babysit for me. I did not have much money to pay anyone to watch my daughter, especially for daycare back then. I also did not trust too many people to watch her. I always thought that I did not want what happened to me to happen to my daughter, so I absolutely trusted nobody but his mom.

One thing about my piece was that we were not equally yoked. I really loved him a lot, but years later we could not come to terms with the church ordeal. I really loved church. After all, it is boring when you are dating someone and have to go to church alone, especially if you are considering being serious with that person. I and my piece went to premarital counseling just to see if we were compatible, and we were.

Then one day I decided to go on a thirteen-day fast with a few friends of mine.

This was my first real fast about something serious. I always knew Mathew 17:21, which says: "Howbeit this kind goeth not out but by prayer and fasting," so I needed clarity for the direction to take moving forward with him. Around my twelfth day of not eating but juicing, my hearing was so clear and eyes were so straight that I could discern anything. This particular Sabbath this pastor spoke about Adam and Eve, and the next thing I knew the man said, "There is someone here who is dating someone, you want them to change, but God wants you to move on and let him do the changing."

I could not believe my ears. Not only did I hear what God told me, so did several others. Always remember 2 Corinthians 13:1: "This is the third time I am coming to you. In the mouth of two or three witnesses shall every word be established." He will always repeat Himself when He wants you to make a move. At any rate, that is how God spoke to me.

Well, I was brokenhearted that I had to tell this guy I was moving on. I think God was tired of my getting it in with this dude. At one point, he really was going to cost me my crown. Fast-forward, I ended up breaking it off with him, and guess what? Shortly afterward he got married.

I was sick. I could not believe he would do such a thing so quickly after our breakup. I remember speaking to him after he got married, and he claimed I did not want him so he married someone who did. Although he was married, he would never tell me the truth. He made it seem as though they were going to get a divorce, but our mutual friend would let me know that he was still married. In a way I felt mad, but then, I was raunchy back then so I couldn't have cared less. I felt like I had him first, and it wasn't my fault that he was stuck with someone he truly did not love just to get back at me.

You ask me how this escapade came to an end. One day, I took my daughter out of town to our spot in the mountains, where I went to get away from life. It almost seemed as if I were running away from myself. It was three hours away from my house and a soothing ride. It seemed like every time I went to this spot and drove around this specific mountain, my cares would disappear. I went to this spot with so many problems and burdens but left with a clear head. It was more like a weekend getaway.

Almost the last day at the spot, I got a phone call from my mom. Out of nowhere she told me to leave my piece alone. I will admit, she knew he was married, that I had some type of fling with him, and that I could not seem to cleanse him from my spirit.

She knew how tight we were at one point, and I remember her saying, "How would you like it if you were married and some other woman was messing or sneaking around with your husband?"

She said the only thing I was connected to in him was a lust demon. Oh my! It was at that moment that I felt totally disgusted at my ways and embarrassed that I would even stoop to a level to trick myself, knowing that although he said he was going to leave her, he really wasn't. Half the time, I could not distinguish if he were honest or lying.

All I know is that at that moment I cried and cried and cried. Finally, God stripped me from him and myself, and I finally felt totally humiliated and sad that I would help someone break the seventh commandment: "Thou shalt not commit adultery." When I pulled myself together, I confessed and asked God to forgive me for my sins and release me from the bondage I was in.

In my mind I was never gay; I just had funny ways about me that I could not understand or control because I used to always think I was a guy. I mean, I'm doing guy things. I had different infatuations when watching porn, but I never acted upon it. I never thought I would bring a female home because I knew my momma wasn't having it even when the friend from school jokingly said one day that we should date. Why did I not catch on then? I always knew right from wrong and always felt I had a good relationship with God although I was off the hook. I mean even when I used to sneak out; I would sit at my window at 12 a.m. and pray to God for protection as I snuck out. Is that not crazy? I'm praying for protection as I am sneaking out the window and have my brains banged out only to come back into my parents' house. I knew what battles not to fight when it came to my parents.

Meanwhile, my friend and I from the teen parenting school

hung out a lot, which is crazy because I did not have many female friends. At one point, I could not stand females and did not know why until the age of twenty-one when I went to counseling due to various struggles and trying to deal with all these different demons I was facing, including drinking, sex, and basic insecurities. This man made me dig so deep that it was painful.

During one session we found out my root issue; and that the true reason I did not feel comfortable with, or like women was because I was molested. This session's revelation explained a lot about the confusion I had growing up. I had no idea that something that happened so long ago could affect my future. It was almost like I swept those situations under the rug by compartmentalizing because I was so young, and I thought it was natural to allow my female cousin to do these things to me. Trying to remember these things was sort of embarrassing, quite difficult, and very uncomfortable. Who wants to admit that they are being sexually abused, and that the abuse caused them to question their sexuality? See, I always had a motto that if I did not go down on a chick, then I'm not gay. You may feel the same way, but truth is that these acts are an abomination to God.

For some reason I would always put myself in these wild and weird situations. For instance, one Saturday night my fiancée from high school and a few of my friends came over to my house to play cards. I clearly remember our drink of choice, vodka straight. I did not care about casually drinking inside my house. After all, I did most of my dirt in the closet, so no one ever knew that I drank, smoked, had various sexual encounters and such because I'm not only a church girl, but a mom singing in the choir and having this perfect fluff life. Keep in mind, I'm not fooling God. He sees everything.

After being tipsy we ended up playing truth or dare, and guess what happened? The girl that I went to the special school with got real wild and finally showed her true colors. Listen, I have never had an experience with the same sex besides what was going on when I was little. I must say that this is one of the worst demons that you can ever fight. At this point, I totally understand the term, "turn you out." I could not believe what just happened, and my fiancé was livid. I was embarrassed because I wasn't expecting any of that foolishness to take place. My guard was totally down, and I regretted drinking that vodka.

Please hear this, my friend; this is one demon you never want to play with. Remember I told you I was into porn? Yes, well, that little escapade did not help because it led me to dig deeper into my selection of what I was watching when it came to porn. Let me not forget adding the girl to other situations with various men. How did I know the girl would end up being involved in my affairs? I forgot to point out earlier that she mentioned she not only wanted to be with me, but when it came down to dealing with my dudes, she would say that she was for me and would do whatever I wanted her to do, pretty much for my pleasure without my having to do anything in return.

I think the dude side of me honestly thought I was pimping

this chick out at one point. Of course, I feel bad looking back because I'm not a dude and because I really felt like she was a really good friend, and because of the drinking that messed up our friendship.

I remember my girl and I going out to this club, dancing with various men until the lights came on. We chugged down a few drinks, and this chick could drink just as many drinks as I could. After the club let out some time in the early morning, we met up with my boyfriend at the time because he lived not too far from the club and because we were too drunk to drive all the way home. We ended up staying at his house. All I can say typing this is, "Lord have mercy because I do not know how we got to his house after we drank so much."

Not to put down skinny girls, but I and the ex whose house we went to always had this saying, "Skinny girls are so extra." So, because the girl wanted to show who she really was and get the after-party between all of us started, I'm sitting there watching her and the boyfriend go at it, and I wasn't even included. That is what I mean by extra. They did not go all the way, but it was enough to make me mad, which later that day caused me and the girl to fall out. We did not speak or see each other for years.

Satan is not clever, but because we are ignorant of his devices, he plays the same games with our emotions, and we allow him to keep scoring. We allow him to use the same tricks. He will put us in a position of vulnerability, and if we allow him, our minds will be screwed to capacity if not gone from watching and participating in devilish things.

In this world, there's a really fine line between good and bad, and it is very scary. This girl and I had a lot in common: we were pretty, had our own places, no baby father to help us out, the same interest in porn sites, same age, both on the grind, kids around the same age, independent, dressed well, had large, close-knit families, got along, never argued, had great conversations, looked out for each other, and always had a side hustle. Why could this not be the perfect relationship if we took it further?

Two reasons. First, I wasn't attracted to her, and second, I would not be able to face God or my parents knowing they weren't having that type of foolishness from me. Also, I had a daughter and did not want to confuse her because I know two woman weren't meant for each other, and I shared this view with that of a well-known psychologist. Most of the time the reason why we have same-sex attraction is either generational curses, someone messed with them at a young age, or some parent made them feel so bad they turned the person off and instilled the feeling of being wanted by the same sex. These things tend to confuse people at a young age. Remember, I thought I was a boy and did not find out until my adult years that a girl molested me. Therefore, this is what caused me to flee from that situation.

Trick Challenge

Have you ever been abused mentally, physically, emotionally, or spiritually? Do you have no one to discuss this serious information with? I challenge you to reach out to a therapist for help. It can be someone that you do not know or someone that you feel very comfortable talking to. I have had a few therapists in my lifetime, and there is nothing wrong with getting help.

2

LOOKING FOR LOVE IN ALL THE WRONG PLACES

My main vice at the time was drinking, and it kept me in all types of bondage and sexcapades. I really should be dead, or my mind should be gone. However, I thank God for grace and mercy because I would not be here without them.One day a girlfriend invited me to a pool party uptown, and you know there was drinking involved. I met some good-looking guy, and the next thing you know I was in his bed. I can't even remember the whole story because of drinking and the simple fact the guy was good-looking. Some guys I could not even tell you their names. I just needed love so bad, and I wasn't going to stop searching for real love until I got it.

One of my main voids was the daddy void. Back then, my dad worked a lot; he was never home because he was always trying to make money to make ends meet. However, we did travel on occasion, sometimes when someone asked my dad and me to sing. I guess you can say we spent time together.

I spent a lot of time with my next-door neighbor's dad because he took the time to be with my brother and me. He allowed us to go bike riding with his children, sledding when it snowed, on vacation with them, going to the water, and maybe taking a dip. When I got older, I looked for that same time in the guys I dated by giving of myself. This made me feel valuable until I got hurt, then I started acting out on the guys and treating them the same way they treated me just because I could.

Oh, let me tell you now about my Jail Ministry era. There was a time when I dated a few drug dealers. One guy in particular would have me make his runs with him at the crack houses. We would get it in while being at the houses, and back then I wasn't really hip to those types of houses. The only thing I knew was it smelled like chitterlings, and I was about to get it in! It was random, spontaneous, and boy, was I stupid. I was oblivious to that atmosphere.

You already know how I feel about guys that put it down; they will have you do anything for them. It was almost like he was feeding me the same type of rock he was selling. There were times when Mr. Hustler would get busted and land his little Black self right back in jail. Of course, I used to go visit, spend my hard-earned money like some of you, and dare somebody to take my visit. I was young and dumb. He definitely had other women coming to see him as well. Come on, I may have been stupid but not that stupid. One time I went to visit him, and the one visit he had was gone. You know what? I ignored it because his brother was funding me to go visit him, and if it weren't for his brother, my daughter and I would not have had our frequent getaways.

Shoot, he not only gave me money for the hotels, but also gas and spending money. I had it sweet, and to be perfectly honest, although I was going to see Mr. Hustler, I still had my piece on the side. I seemed to always have one guy in my back pocket, especially when one did not work out.

There was a time when I took my daughter on a trip with me to see Mr. Hustler, and do you know he proposed to me while in a federal pen? I was like, "Um, get up." I could not take him seriously. Also, his brother had already enlightened me by telling me Mr. Hustler wasn't going to marry me when he got out. I remember going home telling my dad that crap, and guess what he did? He walked away from me, like, girl, please. I'm sure my dad thought about putting his hands around my neck at times for dealing with these knuckleheads and actually planning or even considering marrying a jailbird. I was in love, and we know that word meant lust.

When Mr. Hustler finally came out, he did end up marrying another woman, but it is all good, as he was doing what was expected of him in the first place and at the same time doing me a favor and saving me from lots of headaches.

The other dealer, let's call him Head Honcho. I did not really care about this dude, except that he was one of the top dealers. He was the guy everyone looked up too. When he said go, the clique went; when he chilled, they chilled. He was super outgoing but super wild and crazy. I can't neglect that he liked to spend money on me. Back then, I enjoyed the street life; it was wild, and so was I. We walked hand-in-hand.

I remember taking a trip to New York, and we both had daughters, so this made it kind of fun to travel with them because they were around the same age. It always made things easier staying with a relative. We could save money, and I have a lot of them spread out in New York. This particular time we stayed in the Bronx, not just the ordinary Bronx, I mean the Hood. After settling in, Head Honcho and I decided to leave the girls in the building and step out to the corner store to purchase some liquor and maybe some junk food for the girls. That's right; what good was traveling if you could not drink, smoke, or snack? Let me say that dudes from the District of Columbia at the time did not click with New York dudes at all, for whatever reason. As we walked to the corner store, on the block in front of us there was a gang of at least fifty dudes.

We could see them from a distance holding up their gang signs and saying this loud chant. Then on the other side was another gang of dudes coming. My heart started racing, my knees felt like they were trying to give in on me, and the only thing on my mind was that girls were in the apartment. They had to have been around seven or eight. Plus, I'm thinking how does it look that the only reason I'm in here is to buy something to drink?

Let me tell you, I quickly left Head Honcho in that store. I know that was messed up, but the only thing I could think about was the girls and what would happen if we didn't get back to them because we got shot. I mean, both of us could not die that day in the crossfire, and our girls were waiting for us to return. Especially being in an unfamiliar environment, they would not know what to do. I can tell you this; I did not drink anything that day. I was very grateful that our lives were spared from what went down. Please know I did not wait to stay around to see it.

The day I lost respect for Head Honcho was the day I hung out with him, but I did not know I was tagging along to make his drug drops. I will never forget the time that I saw somebody's mother who did not have any money but wanted some rocks so bad that he threw them on the ground and made her pick them up like a dog eating its first meal and licking it off the ground. She pretty much begged him to give her something. My heart totally melted, but everyone was laughing at this foolishness like it was nothing. This was the day I washed my hands of this dude. I could not be a part of that.

I mean, come on, this is somebody's mother. I felt, nobody could be this heartless that they would treat somebody's momma like this. If he could treat this lady like that, then how was he really going to treat me?

During my tattoo era I got the meanest and craziest tattoos that I know I should not have had put on my body, especially because the body is God's temple. The wild part is, I read the scripture in the Bible about tattoos and still got them. Guess what? I regret every tattoo I have, but back then you could not tell me anything.

My mom did not tell me to not get one; I think it was automatically expected of me to keep my body pure (Leviticus 19:28). I always felt like I had to learn my own lessons and not anyone else's. Truth be told, why would you want to learn your own lessons, especially if someone else had already been through them?

I remember going to Orlando, Florida with a good friend from high school on his business trip. No, we were not dating. He left me in the hotel by myself. Well, why did he do that? For some reason I wasn't scared of anything back then. You want real? This is what drinking will do to you.

After his workday was over, he met up with an old friend. I'm thinking, This dude got me all the way out here with him, and he leaves me in the hotel? Not today! I walked across the street to the Hilton Hotel and met some guy at the bar. Somehow we started drinking, and he told me how he meets this girl at the bar and pays her for sex. That was when I knew I had met the Devil. I was, like, what?

So, shortly after, I meet the girl at the bar. She gets to drinking and ends up telling me her whole operation with the guy, and how much money he pays her to do whatever, and they did this every weekend. I'm not sure if the guy had been married or just looking for pleasure. I do not know how this transpired, but I guess because the guy had a BMW, I assumed he had money. So he asked us what we wanted to do, and he asked if we wanted to go to a strip club.

I was, like, of course, why not? This wasn't my first rodeo at a strip club. I loved going, and, aye, I'm trying to have some fun. I'm from out of town, so why not?

My mistake was that I never reached out to my boy to let him know where I was. I was trying to pay him back for leaving me behind because I was once again in revenge mode, not thinking that this was trick bag mode and anything could've happened.

So we go to the strip club in the hood of Orlando. He rented a private room with at least four ladies, and honestly they weren't worth my money or my time. So, instead of these raggedy strippers getting paid, I ended up getting paid and honestly did not do anything but maybe show some cleavage from what I can remember. I have to be clear, I always wanted to be a stripper because I was great at dancing and knew how to work my mojo and the men's pockets. I had a very strong relationship with the love of money, and by the way, I had a banging body, so I used it to my advantage. I do not know what possessed me to ride in a stranger's car, but looking back, I see I could have been kidnapped, shot, raped, in a terrible accident, sex trafficked, pimped, or shoved into his trunk. I was pretty much riding with Satan, but God and his goodness got me back to their hotel, and although I witnessed some ungodly things between those two demons, I'm just happy God got me back into mine unscathed with a dead cell phone.

I went down to Orlando on business with my homeboy with no money and owed him for paying for my ticket, and by the time we hooked back up I had his money. You know he looked at me crazy, and the only thing I did was smirk at him. You ask yourself, how was she able to come up with her friend's money? What I failed to mention in the beginning of this story was that after the girl gave me her entire operation, she and I were plotting on this dude at the bar. I told her my guidelines; I wasn't having sex, and I wasn't going down on her or him. From what I remember the dude was super dark, had a beer belly and a bald head, and was not attractive at all. I can't remember what the girl looked like, but I told her I would be willing to show myself for a fee and might allow some other things to happen. Fast-forward, I still can't remember how we arrived back to their hotel, but I remembered making the dude seem in my head like he was going to get something from me.

I remember there was an ATM in the hotel, and he wanted to see something, but I told him, "Ah, ah, ah, not until you pay me. Then I will show you whatever."

By the way, I showed but did not have to tell: praise God! They were so drunk I was able to sneak out of that crazy situation, and as God is my witness, I do not know how I made it back to my hotel still half-drunk because we drank shots at the strip club. My homeboy was worried to death about me, and I will never forget how selfish I was that day.

One thing I love and will always love, and I can say it for sure because I'm married, is that sweet, three-letter word: sex! Do not get me wrong, God has always intended sex to be beautiful between a husband and wife, but I did not care. I was insecure, broken, and lonely. I will say one thing that kept me in bondage was that good ole Hennessey and Coke. Yes, yes, sometimes I could drink a whole fifth and not get drunk. Drinking put me in a place of security and happiness, a place to ease my mind from coping with my brother's death and realizing I had been molested. I was also a single parent, and alcohol made me feel secure even though I was very insecure. I just loved the taste of sweet and fire. When you think of it, it doesn't make sense that I would even want to drink something that tastes like fire, but I did. I was hard-headed. I was definitely playing Russian roulette, and Satan was trying to use my vices to kill me and keep me in the trick bag.

There were plenty of days I would go to the club and drive home drunk, not even knowing how I got home without being stopped by a cop, especially in Montgomery County. There were some days I ended up in the wrong bed. Talk about a trick, I was the trick. I told you I loved sex, and I can say that comes from a very passionate place. See, nobody ever really gave me a good talking to about sex. I found out about it from my brother and fast friends in middle school. So of course I was thinking I was having sex, but I was really in lust with demons. When you have true sex, or making love, you are in God's will and doing it God's way so that He can bless it. Yes, the bed is undefiled, and you do not need anything extra. You do not need toys or crazy music. You just need God to bless your worship! That is what this married lady calls sex today.

For years I struggled with trying to do things God's way. Looking back, I see I tried giving up drinking and even tried being abstinent until marriage; each time I gave it up. I cried, but I would go back to both. I would hear a sermon that would touch my heart to give it up, and I cried, yet still I went back. I even went on a fast to find the right kind of guy to date because I was used to dating bum dudes and drug dealers. One day I met someone at a club, and that fast was quickly over after he told me he fixed hearts for a living. I thought, Hey, I struck gold here, and then I told God my fast was over. That night I met the dude; we celebrated with a drink and boom back in bondage. I ended the fast because this man was everything I needed. For one, he was almost a billionaire, and he had, like, fifty grand in his checking account. I know fifty grand doesn't resemble being a billionaire but to me this was a lot of money for only a checking, let alone a savings account. Plus I didn't want to disclose the wads of money he used to have in a box under his bed that I had access too whenever I needed or wanted something (side eye). I have never seen someone with so much money saved at one time that blew my mind. We traveled, we ate at fancy restaurants every day, but doing this also came with a lot of issues. Guess what?

He loved to drink, so somewhere in my mind I knew I could not keep him.

Dating him went against everything that I wanted in a mate, and I was tired of being this monster that my parents did not raise me to be. Although we had sex, I did not feel pleased with him. I do not feel like I pleased him either. I just could not see myself marrying him because for one my daughter could not stand him, and I wanted to make sure that whoever I dated, she liked. Plus I have learned that when you date a man with money, he will play a lot of games and feel entitled to do whatever he wants with your emotions. As a matter of fact, he can buy his way out of anything.

I even put my and my daughter's life on the line one Friday night as we were packing up to go see him to stay the night. I remember clearly. We attempted to leave the house around 7 p.m., and as we made our way into the car, there was another gang moment. On one side of my street in the corner of my eye, I saw a whole gang of dudes carrying pitchforks, baseball bats, and whatever else they had making their way up the street. My heart started racing because this situation took me back to when I was in New York. You probably do not need to guess what I did. I jetted to my door this time not looking back but with the hopes that my daughter was behind me.

Guess what? From my car to the house, it was pitch dark, so I'm sure the gang did not see us, but I silently and with fear called my daughter's name—like, come on, come on.

As she was ducking down, she quickly made a move into our house. Lord, I tell you, if our angels weren't encamped around us, I do not know what was.

This was my first encounter with any gang activity in our area. Although we had a lot of gangs, I had never seen them in such a large group in my area. I met a few Bloods and Crips because they lived across the street from each other, but back then MS-13 was everywhere in my part of town. During the end of me dating Mr. Money, I started trying to scale back on drinking. Mind you, I did not need anybody to drink with me; I would leave work, sneak into the store, buy me some Hennessey and Coke, and mix it in the coke bottle so if I ever got stopped, the cop would not know because he could not smell it on my breath. During the last months, I asked Mr. Money if he would ever stop drinking because I really wanted to stop. I knew if we continued to date, I would never be able to stop. He tried but was powerless. We would go out to eat, and I would step out to use the restroom, and he would sneak a drink, not knowing that I was watching from a distance. At that point, I knew I had to do something. I felt really sad because at one point I thought this was the relationship and I planned no more dating. After all, we all know dating different jokers is exhausting.

I thought we were the perfect couple, but truth be told, I did not know how to fit in with his money game. Yes, I was great at playing the game, knowing how to talk money and spend money, and I was always a great liar. But for the first time in dating history, I lost, although others thought I won.

I wasn't used to dealing with real money. I was used to the dirty drug-dealer money. I could not dress the way I normally dressed. I had to look a certain way in his parents' eyes. I was tired, more like burnt out.

This is a side note for my ladies. If you date a man and your child can't stand them, please flee!

My daughter could not stand this man. I get it now. He would take me on trips, go out to eat, wine and dine me. You know that song, "Nails done, hair done, everything done," and I'm fancy, huh? Yup, that was me, but he never took my daughter with us, and that did not last long. I kept my daughter's feelings in mind.

I remember he went to Miami with his boy and left me behind. So hey, I did the same thing. I was vindictive back then. I needed to clear my head by traveling, so I decided to take a bus to New York to visit my family. I always knew when I traveled, I came back a changed woman. Well, on my way back to Maryland on this never-ending bus ride, the Holy Spirit prompted me to listen to a sermon by a pastor, CD Brooks. Talk about a man of God! This man's sermon was titled "Salt & Fire."

I'm, like, "salt and fire"? What's that about? As I tuned in to what the man of God was saying, the gist of the sermon was saying not to be the one to lose your salvation for some dude. I thought, "Well, another relationship bites the dust." Immediately, I knew I had to break it off with Mr. Money.

The preacher went on to ask, "How would you feel if your

family was on the inside of the Heavenly City, smiling and watching you, and you're on the outside all because of one man?" I knew I could not take that chance of jeopardizing Heaven for one person. I thought of meeting up with my brother again and seeing relatives whom I lost in the past.

So, I thought to myself, God you do not have to tell me twice. I know for a fact God was speaking to me.

I called the guy and told him we had to meet. I think he kind of felt my vibe and figured I was coming over to say it was over. I tried to break it off with him one time before, but it did not work, and I ended up staying in the trick bag. Meanwhile, we met at his house, and before I said what I had to say he asked me one question. "If we got married, would I be able to drink occasionally?"

I said no because I did not want the main bondage, drinking, to make me feel guilty every day. That is torture, especially considering my history of crying whenever I thought about giving up drinking.

Always remember one thing about the enemy and this trick bag ordeal: he knows how to speak your language, and at the time my main language was money. Check this out. The money dude said that if we got married, he would take care of everything including loans, and back then I was making good money. I was bringing home two grand biweekly after taxes. I asked myself, Well, what would I do with my check?

He said to put it toward my daughter's private school education, which was only $400 a month, and use it for us as spending money when we traveled. I thought this was too good to be true, and I asked myself if I would honestly marry him just to get my student loans paid off.

Do not judge me. If you had this offer presented to you, you would think about it, maybe even marry the man and fake the funk. I know God would not bless me for doing that. So, you see, I had a heart deep down under all that concrete.

I think I would have been too miserable to even survive that marriage. I mean, let's be clear; whenever you invest time in a relationship, it is never easy to break that off. I'm not being insensitive to my situation; it was hard. We spent a lot of time together. We had decent talks. We had the best vacations every month, and we ate at the best spots.

I'll talk about the vacations quickly. We went to Miami once a month, and, of course, we had to hit up Wet Willie's on the strip. Talk about the trick bag! Miami's strip is no spot for someone trying to let go of drinking. We went shopping at the outlets and even some of the best boutique shops that cost an arm, a leg, and a kidney. I remember him paying to get one of my tattoos covered to meet his momma, which was a rip-off because the tatt was the size of a quarter and they charged over $100 at Miami Ink. I only got a tatt of a one heart and a few small music notes (representing my love of music). I could live with my tatt choice since I sing.

I do not remember getting in the water. I can vaguely remember going to the Camelot. Before we even got inside, there was a fight, and after we walked in, there was another fight! I immediately felt that going to this club was the wrong move, especially since before meeting this guy I had not stepped into a real club for some years. I remember drinking the entire time until the club closed and staying at his peep's vacation spot on the other side of town. Mind you, I have no idea how we got home that morning. I just remember being so drunk and finally arriving at the spot in West Palm Beach. I opened the door and fell out of the car onto the ground. I do not even know how we both got in the house, and this was a pretty rich and clean neighborhood. I simply have to believe our angels drove us home shaking their heads at us and interceding with Jesus Christ on our behalf the entire ride.

I remember going to Jamaica and arriving mid-morning. Of course, my motto was, "What is a vacation without drinking, right?" I remember staying at one of the best four-star, all-inclusive Sandals resorts and drinking my beverage of choice for breakfast and then having the nerve to go zip lining. What was I thinking? I was super wild, but I did not care. I felt free, and I did not regret a thing. I was in another country; this was my break from the world; leave me alone. I do not even think I thought about God on this trip. I drank the entire time I was there.

So you mean to tell me this relationship wasn't hard to let go? All the fun we had together? After I told him we were unequally yoked and that I wanted God to bless our relationship, he told me something that I will never forget. He said, "If you ever need anything, help with your daughter's schooling or money, call me." Then he gave me that goodbye kiss on the forehead.

Although a deep, almost lump-like feeling was in my throat, my response was, "Before you, God took care of us, and after you God will continue to take care of us."

I often smile at the faith that I had in that very moment. I know God was smiling down on me because after that moment, my life went nothing but uphill from that point on. Do not get me wrong. I'm not saying that having a breakup isn't challenging and that there won't be rainy days or dim days. I'm saying God will put you in the perfect position to be with whom He wants you to be.

Trick Challenge

If you feel you are in a serious relationship, and you think you might marry this person but are confused about whether you should be in a relationship at all, do what I did. Write a list of similarities and differences. If the good outweighs the bad, it may work, but if the bad outweighs the good, kindly sweep them into the trick bag, or you will end up getting tricked!

3

MORTIFYING YOUR FLESH

Before my breakup, I jotted down a few notes in my diary. Yes, I kept a diary; it was my way of expressing to God and pouring out to Him everything I was carrying on my shoulders. Although there was plenty of gossip in that diary, there were lots of prayers and questions I had for God. I discussed my struggles, doubts, and things I needed Him to help me understand, and I talked to God just like I'm talking to you like a friend.I appreciate my diary; it was my guideline for writing this book and truly expressing my feelings at that specific time until the present.

Guess what? All of my entries started with, "Dear God!" I wanted to be as open with God as I could. Before I broke up with Mr. Money, I wanted to compare our similarities and then our differences. I had seventeen similarities and thirty-three differences, which meant the bad outweighed the good. I also took a short trip to clear my head so that I would have time to think about my decision before bluntly breaking it off. According to my diary, I had broken up with him months before the final breakup.

Some of you are going through this challenge as I speak. You do not know if you should keep your partner because you think you love them. Remember, you cannot let your emotions stand in the way of following your gut feelings: compare, contrast, sweep, or keep.

Breaking up with Mr. Money was difficult. Although I knew God wanted me to end that relationship, I was really hurting. I hated dating. It seemed like every promising relationship I entered had things always backfire on me. Then I had to realize I wasn't the only person involved. Our kids were involved. I started to regret my decision, and through it all, I still talked to God, and I still trusted God.

I even have a certain excerpt in my diary that read:

May 15, 2011, 12:12 a.m.

> God, I trust you. Even though, me and Mr. Money departed, You have the last say so. We both have grown apart because of being unequally yoked, but I thank you, God, for peace and a hug.

There were days when I wondered if I had made the right choice to break it off with him. No matter what, I always thanked God that He knew what I needed. I asked Him to continue to work with me as a young lady. I constantly thanked Him for a great night's rest because my spirit was uneasy. I thanked Him for my testimony that He would give me to come back and write about, and, boy, did He give me something to write about!

You will read that in the upcoming chapters. If you feel dejected or hopeless, do not get it twisted. This is something that each and every one of you reading this book will encounter if you're not wise about whom you're dating and if you don't consult God prior to entertaining anyone's so-called relationship.

It is essential to ask God whom He wants you to court before you decide to move forward, or you will mess with the tricks and end up in the trick bag. Why do we need God? Well, for starters, He's all-knowing and wise, and He is the creator of everything. He's the one Who will save us the extra fat bags under our eyes and will keep us from bondage. Oh, let's talk about bondage, and then we will touch back on prayer.

Bondage is the trick bag. The trick bag is any vice that keeps us in bondage. Bondage is like witchcraft; it will put a spell on us every time. Bondage is an addiction. Bondage is like a pimp, and we know pimps do not love us. They want to beat us, use us, and have us strung out, and when the fun is over, they want us to repay them for everything we made. We work hard for pimps. We keep money in their raggedy pockets. That mean witch called bondage will keep us locked into our sins and spellbound for life if we allow it. When you think of this scenario, this is insane, right? Lord Jesus, please help us.

Let's go a little deeper. Have you ever read the definition of a masochist? It is someone who seeks pleasure from the infliction of pain or humiliation. Have you ever met someone who practiced such humiliation? Oh, let me answer that for you. Yes, I just raised my hand. That is how I got all my tattoos, from pain and humiliation. Wow, I was a masochist at one point minus the sexual nonsense. I did not know how to deal with my pain, so guess what? I got my first tattoo, and this crap hurt and was not pleasurable. After all, who wanted ten or more baby needles plucking and digging in their skin for hours? Yup, I found my new outlet. I not only got my first high, tinkering in the tattoo world, but every time I went through something crazy in my life, I was back in the chair for a tattoo. You know the trick bag can have us acting real stupid out here in these streets. I tatted a guy's name on my back, trying to show my loyalty to him and how much I loved him only to get it covered later on in life. SMH (shaking my head)! If a guy does not tat your name on him, I do not care how much he tells you he loves you, please do not be extreme like me and tat his name on you. I do not care how good the sex is; it is all lust, and when you have sex outside of marriage (God's will), you are now enjoining with demonic spirits.

When I got hurt or went through a breakup or something life-changing, guess what I got? You got it, another tattoo. Although I have plenty of tattoos, this did not and will not define who I am or where I am spiritually with God. It showed where my mindset was at the time. God tells us to come out of the world. I neglected to mention right before I got my first tattoo, my girl showed me in the Bible how we aren't supposed to put markings on our bodies, and I still neglected God's instruction for my body. Leviticus 19:28 says, "Ye shall not make any cuttings in your flesh for the dead nor print any marks upon you: I am the Lord."

As I got older and my walk with God became more serious, I regret marking my body, especially when I sang at various churches. I started feeling ashamed because the people looked down on me and made me feel bad, in particular when I was struggling with maintaining my relationship with God. Today, I'm not ashamed of my crazy experiences. I will say that each and every tattoo represents the story of my pain, as well as my past. Although some people can't digest the fact that I had a past, as we all have, we need to learn to lay down each and every dilemma at the foot of the cross and stop sharing our business and depending on people to deliver us. Last, I remember there was only one Savior who died and is the judge of us. One thing about Jesus, He died for us, not people who can't do anything for us.

I think I have always enjoyed praying. Keep in mind, when I used to sneak out during the wee hours of the morning, there I was sitting at my window like Daniel looking and counting the stars with the window open, gazing up into the Heavens, smelling that fresh midnight air, praying and talking to God as if the place that I was traveling to was going to please Him. Oh yes, somebody was going to get pleased, but it wasn't God. What was I thinking? Every night I had my all-black outfit all picked out so that nobody would notice me, wishing to blend in with the trees and black asphalt. I boldly asked God for protection, asking Him to cover me as I was religiously sneaking out and praying that I wouldn't someday get caught. I snuck out three months straight. I do not know what I was thinking. You know I could have gotten into a serious car accident coming and going, and to think this never crossed my mind. You know, we really serve a merciful God, a God who gives us chance after chance and opportunity after opportunity. We serve a God who in His grace gives us time and space to repent, so we can one day come to ourselves and return to Him. We also serve a God who has no problems chastising His children. You may feel like you are so far gone that God wants nothing to do with you. Wrong. I'm reminded of Hebrews 13:6: "For whom the Lord loveth he chasteneth and scourgeth every son whom he receiveth."

Lord, if I only knew then what I know now. After months of sneaking out, guess how I got caught? An angel snitched on me by leaving the front door open, and mind you, I used to sneak out my window. Talk about Grace and Mercy. So early one evening as I was planning my usual night out on the town with the guy I was dealing with at the time, here comes my mom accusing me of sneaking out the front door. She says, "You saw that boy last night didn't you?"

I looked at her and said, "No!" I was lying through my teeth, but telling the truth because I used to go out my window.

I would never be that bold to walk out the door, the front door at that.

She smacked me in the face and yelled, "Liar!"

I could not believe she did that. Why did she have to smack me in the face? Sheesh, a mother's wrath!

Then here it goes. I sharply commented, "I did not walk out the front door. I went out my window." As I was walking back to my room, she got in my face and then on top of me, like "Oh, you grown? I dare you to hit me."

Let me tell y'all this, I do not care how mad my mom got, even fussing in my face to the point where her nose is touching mine, I never thought about raising my finger to her. I stand by Ephesians 6:1, "Children obey your parents in the Lord for this is right." I do not care how off the hook I was. I was furious, and after she pulled that move that was the last straw for me. I closed my door, kept it unlocked so they could see I left, lifted my window, and rolled out. I wasn't going back this time. I needed to cool off. I decided to go to my friend's house that was about five houses down the street. I knew for sure she and her mom would help me after they heard my story.

Although I snuck out for months, for some reason, that night was a little unusual. I was a little scared to walk in the deep darkness. It was late, and I was super mad, and we all know when we are mad nothing matters. I mean nothing. Here I am standing on the doorstep of my friend's house and banging hoping they would open the door quickly because I was scared, only to find a 12-gauge shotgun facing me, and just like that I could have been blown away. That would have been a good time to do it while I was running wild on Satan's path doing my own thing and not God's. Once again, God's grace and mercy sustained me and kept me that night. Meanwhile, my friend's mom saw me and said, "Girl, you better be lucky; you almost got shot banging on my door like that." She asked me, "Why are you not home?"

I respond by telling her what happened and instead of her taking me in, guess what she did? Called my parents and told them to come pick me up.

My mom asked her, "What do you mean? Teshawn is in her room!" Oh boy, how embarrassing. They go to my room only to find the door unlocked, me not there, and my window up after I just got in trouble for sneaking out. I wasn't thinking. I was young and did not care about anything. Now we have two dilemmas; not only am I mad but embarrassed because my plan backfired on me. My parents pulled up giving me that cold embarrassing stare, and talk about God chastising us. My momma got out of the car, looked at me, and said some words I will never forget, "If you ever sneak out your window again, I will send you away to a military school until you turn eighteen."

Well, folks, that did it for me. From that day forward I never snuck out again. I have been praying since I was a little girl and always felt connected to Jesus. I do not care how many sins I have committed, what I do know is that Jesus has always heard and answered my prayers. I do not recall all the details because I was seven at the time, but I do remember riding with my grandparents to Georgia to help move my aunt into her new place. It was a hot day, and we finally moved our last load from the U-Haul. As we rushed out of grandpa's car, we locked the door behind us not, realizing the key was left in the ignition. Grandpa had one of those automatic locks with the code on the ledge of the door but could not figure out the code. By this time everyone's hysterical trying to pry their way into unlocking the door. I silently intervened and said, "We did not pray." So I said a prayer believing that Jesus would hear and answer by unlocking the door, and as soon as we said, "Amen," the door unlocked. I will never forget this story. It is very near and dear to my heart because I was so young and God had answered a little girl's prayer. I would like to say this was my first miracle!

Weeks after I broke it off with Mr. Money, my mom asked me to join the prayer line, and I know this was the beginning of my becoming a skilled prayer warrior. Why do I say this? I'm glad you asked. It was one of the first steps of my overcoming myself. Not only did she ask me to take the line, she asked me to take the 6 a.m. hour. Give a drumroll, praise, and worship! I immediately got excited because I absolutely love to testify, but then I got scared. I thought it would be too much commitment for me. I did not want to disappoint the administrator and couldn't fulfill my role. Let's go over my anxiety. For one, I was a single parent with multiple jobs. I already had problems with getting up in the morning. I'm not a morning person. I was due to work at 7 a.m., so how am I going to write down these people's prayer request, talk, and drive at the same time?

Even worse, you want me to do 6 a.m? I rehearsed all of this in my mind. This also meant I would have to wake up earlier than 6 a.m. to have personal worship and figure out the topic of discussion for that hour. Well, I will tell you this. When you have good intentions and you want to take your mind off of yourself and place all of your efforts on someone else, please know God will provide and take care of everything, especially when your heart is in the right place. I never felt so fulfilled. By taking on the prayer line, I met so many wonderful people and still have a diary of their prayer requests from when I interceded on their behalf.

God knew exactly what He was doing by putting me on a more consistent regimen. There were some days when I did not know what I was going to talk about. I just prayed for that whole hour. I prayed for anything and everything. I prayed for some of the old callers' requests from previous days. Some days, it felt lonely with no one talking on the line. There would be silent callers just listening, but they would not submit a request. I would bust out with a session of prayer, and sometimes I got so caught up into praying I forgot to open the line back up for someone who needed prayer. I also remember spirits trying to come on the line and take over or trying to interrupt. Taking on that task was no joke because you could not intercede on the behalf of folk any kind of way. You really had to walk upright so you would not be hypocritical trying to get a prayer through, so I thought.

I mean, let's consider the priests in the Old Testament (Leviticus 10:3-7). On the Day of Atonement there were very strict rules as to what the priest could and could not do, so I really did not take the prayer line lightly. I thought it was a big role that needed to be filled. I had so many issues. I think I had enough to pray about, and that would exceed that hour. I had enough issues to pray over for the entire year. I remember constantly praying for my drinking habit that God would rid me of it and asking God to heal my hurt and pain and to help me. I really do believe I stopped drinking during the time I took the line. I do not remember, but I know God did not forget this prayer. I took this prayer line for thirty days just to get my feet wet, and I was consistent. I did not miss a day even on the weekend. I would work my plans around this prayer line because it started becoming a part of my life. I liked it so much that when it was time to end the line I ended up taking the evening 6 p.m. line on praise and worship.

Trick Bag Challenge

Are you going through and do not know how to get through it? I challenge you to take on someone else's problems by sowing into them and uplifting them and maybe do something nice for them and let them know you care.

4

RECOGNIZE
WHOSE YOU
ARE

After many months on the prayer line, I finally got over
Mr. Money. I gained some self-worth because I was tired of
putting myself in these crazy situations. You know, sometimes you get tired of chasing after the same sorry people,
tired of being heartbroken, and then you finally see you
are what some may call desperate. That is when you realize
you're in a good place, almost like going to AA. In order to
work through your addiction, you have to admit you're an
alcoholic. My heart was finally moving toward the end of
my healing phase. I was ready to move on and date myself
and my daughter again with no distractions. Although I was
working toward moving forward and dying to myself, I still

felt this empty spot in my life that needed fulfillment. I was still trying to overcome drinking and feel good things, so I got this bright idea to find some help. I needed counseling. I did not want any counselor. I needed a specific counselor.I did not want a counselor who knew me because I did not want anyone looking at me sideways or going back to discuss my business with anyone. I was on the hunt for a psychiatrist who would tell me what I needed to hear. I was filled with so many spirits that nobody could relate. There was a point in time where one of my mentors, who is also a pastor, invited me to his house to lay hands on me because I had so many spirits. It was horrible. It reminded me of the scripture in Mathew 12:45, where it states that if you return to your old way of living or go back to the addiction that you dropped, your last state is worse than the first. Trust me. Every time I thought I got the victory over something or someone, but then I returned back to it or them. It was true; the state of me became worse. I can see how people become crazy. They start losing their minds and doing crazy things.

I have to say, God is patient, and one day his cup of patience will be full. Revelations 22:11: "He that is unjust, let him be unjust still: and he which is filthy, let him be filthy still: and he that is righteous, let him be righteous still: and he that is holy, let him be holy still."

During my wilding out moments, I remember searching for this scripture and could not find it to save my life. I desperately needed help. I was drowning in misery. I was needy and had no hope. I did not want to share with anyone. I felt isolated. I do not care how many prayer lines I took, I still had this bondage hovering over me on a daily basis. Although I took on others' situations by praying for them, I could not see the light at the end of my own tunnel.

One Friday night, one of my cousins and some of my friends came over. This night was different from all the other nights. One reason was because it was the Sabbath, and I always felt like drinking or clubbing was forbidden on the Sabbath. It seemed like we purchased every alcohol under the sun and beer. I can remember this beer. It looked like an energy drink. It was one of those drinks that had you up all night.

Oh, we partied that night, and the most unusual thing happened. One of my girls was in town and dropped by to say hello, but in the process she walked to her car to smoke a jay. Do you know as much as I hated smoking jays, I walked outside as drunk as I was, opened her passenger door, and hit that jay. We did not get much sleep that night, but we ended up attending the church right down the street from my house the next morning, and I was on time. Funny, because months back my cousin was making plans to get baptized so all of our family and friends wanted to attend when she did, and I wanted to get baptized again.

You would not believe what happened next. I have to say our God has a personality. We serve a clever God, a God who knows what we like and will let us go all-in before we give up ourselves. The pastor was preaching on the same scripture that I was searching months for. He talked about the seven spirits that enter back into you after you give that thing up but return back to your bondage. Oh my, when the sermon was over, he made an altar call and opened the doors of the church. I told my cousin, "Listen, I know you want to get baptized with me and the family wants to come and support you, but I just have to get into that pool."

I told her how I made a vow to God that if He opened a swamp for baptism, I would jump in. Well, ladies and gents, this was my swamp moment. I swiftly made my move to the front so the pastor could recognize my decision. Shortly after that I made my way to the back to get changed to jump in that pool of mercy. Wouldn't you know it? My cousin was right behind me to take that step with me. Matter a fact, she ended up in the water with me, and I thought that was a big deal because here she was a devoted Catholic young lady, getting baptized into a Seventh-day Adventist Church. Wow!

I thought that was a big step for her, and at the same time when I went down in the water that day, I came up as a new creature in Christ. I can honestly say that when I went down, my life never was the same again, and it did change for the good. For the first time, I finally felt free.

I can attest that there is definitely something to that water baptism. I felt like Paul after he got finished persecuting the Christians and God had to step in. He sent him to meet Barnabas, and after Barnabas said those words to Paul the scales fell off his eyes. Well, the scales fell off my eyes because I could see, and I felt brand new. I felt that all of those things that haunted me prior to going down in the water fell off in the water. My discouragement, addictions, and bondages all disappeared, and I came up brand new.

After I came up the pastor pushed me to the microphone in the water, and I will admit I was scared because I did not want to be electrocuted by singing in the water, but I sang my song, "I want Jesus to walk with me," and He did! No wonder I could not find a psychiatrist. God was walking with and counseling me all along.

After I got baptized again on September 24, 2011, my life has never been the same, and I never drank, smoked, or had pre-marital sex again. I have to include that my aunt also played a role in coaching me to stay alcohol-free. She too was an alcoholic, so she knew how to coach me through this next phase in my life. I forget the exact day I gave up drinking, but I will say she was truly there for me. I remember something else she said that stuck with me like glue. She said, there will be good days as well as bad days, but the good outweighs the bad, and as you move forward in your walk with Christ, it will become easier. I stand here to say it became easier. I did not put much thought to drinking, but I will say God told me if I kept drinking, He would allow the devil to take me out of here. So that was a detailed instruction for me and I listened.

Eighteen days following my baptism, I got a message on Facebook from some random guy. My daughter was sitting beside me when I reviewed his profile. You know what they say about people on Facebook: they are crazy. I didn't want to entertain anybody crazy. So I was very careful about dealing with this guy. After all the messages before his, I got scared because I was pushing God on them to see who was who and they ran off. Anyhow, she and I were trying to guess what he was because he had a mic to his mouth on his profile. I thought a poet, singer, or rapper, so I reviewed his message and it said:

I do not usually do this, but I was at a loss for words when I laid my eyes on your pics. If you're as beautiful on the inside as you are on the outside, then I would love to get to know you if you're not already occupied with anyone else. I love that you are into church. Call me or text me, 301.xxx.xxxx. God bless.

My response was, Amen. To God be the glory. I'm not occupied with anyone. The only loves of my life are Jesus Christ and my daughter. I'm just trying to fall in love with Him and stay connected, so I will have discernment. And when the right man comes along, I will know how to treat him. Pouring into my daughter. At the end of the day, she's the only soul that matters.

I have no idea how this guy was able to view anything on my page, but apparently he was following my devotionals through mutual friends. Listen, you have got to understand that after the breakup with Mr. Money, I did not want any more disappointments. Plus, I vowed to God that I would no longer put Him on the shelf and if I ever ended up dating again, He would get to choose the mate. I couldn't forget because I just got baptized. I was new to this particular church, I'm the hottest commodity there, and I also assumed that I was going to be a pastor's wife. Now that I'm thinking about it, I'm not sure if I could have handled that task. Only Jesus knows what our pastor's wives go through.

I had good intentions. The main reason I wanted to be a pastor's wife was so I would not have to worry about the pressure of having sex outside the sanctified boundaries of marriage, going back to drinking, and my mouth would be completely clean from cursing. Plus, I would be more focused spiritually, and he would help me out with my relationship with God, more like an accountability partner.

Let's call the new guy, Mr. Facebook. As I started attending the church I just got baptized at, I started making friends, becoming totally submerged in church activities. I also started hanging with one of my girls from back in the day who attended that church as well. Aye, I was single and trying to mingle, and she was single, so we started hanging every week. During this time, she also met Mr. Facebook, and no matter how much this guy tried to pursue me or get next to me, I would shove him off because, as I told my girl, I only wanted to have a platonic friendship with him and prove to my other friends that I could date myself for at least a year. The girl ended up inviting him out to hang with us.

Then, I will never forget, I invited him to my house. I have no idea why because he was a stranger and I did not know him from Adam, but I guess I felt safe because my girl was in the service. So if he tried something I'm sure all three of us, to include my daughter, could take him. Our first attempt at inviting him over was during the week, but since he did not have a car, he had to catch public transportation. So, he called around 9:30 p.m. stating he was on his way. Remember, I am a new creature now, so my rules had changed and I no longer entertained late-night company. I kindly told him he would not be coming to my house at 9:30 p.m. I believe I had to work, plus it wasn't becoming for a young woman to have company around this time of night. I forget who used to say this but they always said, "Ain't nothing open after 10 p.m. but legs."

I really held on to this saying after my conversion. During one of my and Mr. Facebook's conversations, we were trying to figure out how he was going to come to the house. I mentioned how he should come and bring in the Sabbath with us, which starts Friday sunset and ends Saturday sunset, this is how God created the earth, from sunset to sunset. During one of our talks, I introduced the Sabbath to him as family time and a time to catch up with God and each other. During this time we usually eat, play spiritual games, have spiritual discussions, go out in nature, and dedicate the entire twenty-four hours to be centered on God, doing God things. I also mentioned to him that I throw down in the kitchen, and I'm sure he was pretty happy about that. I love to cook, and because none of my friends cooked full-course meals like me, my house was always full and was the go-to spot to eat every Friday night. Also, you know what they say: food is the way to a man's heart.

I did invite him over the next day, and he brought in the Sabbath, and this time he came earlier. When he arrived, he was a nice height, but had tats all over his arms, which was something I did not want. He wore earrings in both ears, and he had pretty nice hands that were attractive to me. He wore shorts that day, but I wasn't crazy about his legs (and I'm a legs person), but overall he was cute. I noticed something different about him from all the other guys; my daughter was super nice to him. Her hospitality was out of this world from the time he arrived until the time he left. I have never seen her act so kindly to any of my guy friends except for him. She offered him something to drink. I mean, she served him, and that was something that opened my eyes. When I tell you my daughter did not like anybody, that is what I mean.

I had a nice list of guys at one point. After Mr. Facebook came over to eat, he asked me if he could go with me to church. I told him I did not know about coming with me to church but sent him to attend a church in Virginia, and because my parents attended that church, he would have the opportunity to get to meet them. Let's keep in mind, I just got baptized and I'm now thinking I'm going to be a pastor's wife, and I'm also keeping this a platonic relationship, plus I did not want to be seen with anybody new. I was the new kid on the block.

Guess what? Mr. Facebook attended that church I sent him to, but he did not run into my parents. Guess who he did meet? God! Whatever that pastor preached that day made that man take both his earrings out of his ears.

Later on after church he ended up coming back over my house to discuss what the pastor was talking about and how he was in the pew taking out his earrings, and at the time I was still wearing mine, I was, like, I wish I could hear a sermon so powerful that would make me take mine out! Although I did not want anyone coming with me to church, the very next week, Mr. Facebook started attending church with me and my daughter. The conversation between me and Mr. Facebook ended up being an everyday thing.

During my first conversations with Mr. Facebook I noticed he had a big problem: his mouth was worse than a sailor. Then I noticed he would talk to me about God, but at the same time he dropped some big words, I mean the F-bomb and the B-bomb. I was, like, this can't be the man God has for me. I automatically thought he was trying to play the game with me. I was, like, Satan sent this dude to be a distraction and get me off my spiritual path.

The next week came, and we were emailing and texting all day. I would be at work and he would ask me questions like, "What are your views on sex?"

I would say, "God says, 'Sex is meant for marriage.'" Then he would ask me questions about different views, and I mean every answer I responded to I would send him a quote from Scripture to back up God's word. I wasn't playing any games this time around, and because guys would reach out to me on Facebook prior to him reaching out, they would ask me questions similar to his and I would respond based on God.

Well, those dudes would say, "I'm sorry. I'm not on your level. Have a great life."

Nope, not Mr. Facebook! Mr. Facebook was asking me all these questions but at the same time was getting reeled in like a fish caught on a hook.

All of this was unintentional on my part because I did not put any thought into him. My girlfriend was the one stating we should hang out with him. I guess she was trying to pursue him. The more I ignored him, the more he was attracted to me. Another reason why I wasn't putting any thought into this guy was because, according to my diary and the things I wanted in a man, he did not qualify because he wasn't a Christian. He also did not have a car, still lived with his parents, and did not have a good job. Nope, not my cup of tea. I needed someone who was on my level mentally, spiritually, and emotionally; however, we had great conversations, and I really enjoyed them. I looked forward to those conversations.

During one of our talks, I asked him if he kissed his mother with that mouth, and he thought about it, like, yes? I really could not believe how foul it was, but he eventually toned it down. One day, one of my girls, Mr. Facebook, and I went out on a date to Vapianos, this wonderful Italian spot. Yes, I would say this was our first official date among all three of us. Remember, she was in the service, so she was the third party of protection, and it was wonderful.

We all had a good time getting to know Mr. Facebook.

Then all of a sudden, My piece called me out the blue. Oh no, you got to know when to tell the devil, "Not today."

I sternly told my piece that I was about to get married and to never call me again. Not that I was about to get married, I was angry with him and frustrated because he lied so much about his not being married. Furthermore, I was a new creature in Christ; the old things were done away, and so was my past. I'm here to say he never called me again.

The next week, I invited Mr. Facebook out to my second parents' surprise birthday party, and because I was the girl they never had, they asked me to be a waitress, and my brothers were the waiters. I figured I would bring him to the function so I could see how he would get along with others without my being next to him. Then he could not only meet my parents, but also my second parents and my extended brothers.

After the party was over and he got in the house, I got this text from him, something like, I had a good night. I love you.

"I love you?" Um, we weren't even an item, and this dude is in love already? I was scared. You know what they say about guys on social media? They are serial killers. Crazy, all of these outlandish but true things were going through my mind.

I never responded to him because I thought that was weird and I was trying my best to be single; plus, it was too early for this dude to be saying, "I love you." I had an appointment with my naturopathic doctor one day during that week due to some health challenges. My doctor all of a sudden tells me to share with him what was going on with my health. I was, like, why? I do not like him. She said that is fine if you do not like him, but he's pursuing you. I immediately thought I needed to go run and tell this dude what was going on with me. I called him up and said I needed to meet him ASAP. I was in DC, and he was in Virginia.

He told me, "OK, come on."

I rushed out there to meet up with him, and guess what ended up happening? I met his parents that day. I knocked on the door, and his dad opened the door. You know what was weird? I never called his parents "Mr. and Mrs. Logan." I always called them Mom and Dad from the beginning. You have to know that this situation was divine due to how everything came together. After meeting his parents, we stepped outside to go for a walk so we could talk. In his neighborhood, they had this nice pond and a cute, little posh gazebo. We sat in the gazebo, and it was there our history together began.

At first, I hesitated to tell him why I came so far to meet him. Everything was moving at such a fast pace, and I honestly was not trying to date him. I only wanted a friendship. I discussed what was going on with my health and the different concerns.

He asked, "That is it?"

I mean, that was a big burden lifted off of me, to hear him

say that. It seemed like my health situation at one point was taking a toll on me. He thought I was coming down to break things off with him, which is crazy to me because we did not have anything but a friendship.

Then he said, "I have something to ask you as well."

Remember, I told you he might be a rapper? I failed to mention that he was a part of his family's entertainment label. He was a vicious rapper, I must admit. I heard some of his music, and it was nice, better than some of these rappers in the industry. He had an awesome vocabulary as well.

Getting back to the story, he finally asked me the question: "Will you be able to come out and support me at the club?"

Club? Boy bye. I'm saying all this in my mind. I haven't been in a club for years, and please do not think I'm going back to that now. I calmly told him, "I do not go to clubs, and haven't been for years."

I mean, I could not lie, Mr. Money and I went to one in Miami, and that was a few months back, so I did not want to slip back into that trick bag. You know the buck had to stop here. I had enough, one minute he was talking about God, the next minute he was cursing, and now you want me to go support you at a club? I said, "Either you are going to serve God or you are going to serve Satan, and whomever you choose, serve them to the fullest." When we finally ended our conversation I gave him something to think about.

That night I talked to God and decided to go on a fast for clarity in regard to what He wanted with my life. Things seemed to be moving so quickly, and I wasn't in the mood to have my emotions toyed with again. My prayer was simply this, "Lord, you know I'm tired of going through the motions with these guys. I do not want to play any games, I promised you I would not put You on the shelf and date anyone without you again. If this guy is not meant to be in our lives, remove him tomorrow."

The very next day I get a call from Mr. Facebook. He says, "I thought about what you said, and I do not want to serve Satan to the fullest. I do not want to lose what we have, and I quit the label."

Shocked, I said, "Good. So does that mean you accept God as your personal Lord and Savior?"

He said, "Yes."

I said, "OK, repeat after me the sinner's prayer and mean it."

So he said, "Dear God, I know that I am a sinner. I am truly sorry for my sins. I believe that Jesus is the Son of God, that He died on the cross to pay for my sins, and that He rose again and is interceding in Heaven for us. I ask You now, Jesus, to forgive my sins, and to come into my life and save me. Help me to live for You. I ask this in Jesus' name, Amen."

I told him, "Believe that God heard you and saved you!"

You know, I really felt like he believed because after he

repeated this prayer and accepted Jesus to come into his heart, his life was never the same again. He never cursed again, drank, or went out again, and he really did quit his label.

After he called me my fast was immediately over. God had answered my prayer overnight. Prior to his calling me to tell me he did not want to lose what we had, it seemed like I believed God was really going to move this guy. The very next morning I dialed the twenty-four-hour prayer line to testify as to what God did with my friend. A prophetic pastor was in charge on the 5:30 a.m. line so his line was full and jumping every day. Sometimes you could barely get a prayer through because so many people bombarded him during his prayer hour.

The morning I called he opened the line for testimony, or prayer and I patiently waited for no one to say anything, and they did not, so I quickly said, "Please pray for my friend. He just accepted Jesus Christ as his Lord and Savior the other day."

Out of nowhere, the pastor said, "The Holy Spirit wanted me to tell you he's going to be your husband."

I was like, what? I honestly did not believe that man until he said this, "And He also wanted me to let you know he's proud of you."

It wasn't until that very moment, I fell to my knees, prostrate, crying like a close relative had just died because I honestly felt like God had forsaken me and he wasn't paying attention to my sacrifices. I felt like God did not see everything I had given up just to follow Him. I mean, drinking? Really? Like, I felt that was one of the hardest things that I ever gave up, and for God to be proud of me was a big deal.

You want to know something? After the pastor told me that, from that morning forward my attitude and feelings toward Mr. Facebook started changing a little. After all, I kind of spoke things into existence when my piece had reached out to me.

Oh boy, since he was going to be my husband, I had to see if he were serious about dating me. I wanted to do something different and test out courting. I advised him to ask my parents if they would approve. I knew this would give my mom something to talk to her friends about because this time around this guy was different.

For some of you who are not familiar with the term "court," it means no sex, no kissing, no private dating. Most of our dates were centered around family and friends, so we would not be tempted to make some moves. Plus, courting is for those who are sure they are going to marry. More like speed dating, if you will, if you were considering that route during the courting phase. Oh my, I lied. I thought drinking was one of the hardest things to give up. Nope, sex was one of the hardest things by far during this process to not partake in, especially when we started spending more and more time together.

You start to connect mentally instead of physically, but it is a different attraction that you start to have. You start connecting to God through that person and the God attributes. I think for me the hardest part was when God told me not to do anything sexual. God gave me specific directions in courting him. God told me if we had sex we were not going to get married, and I would not be able to complete my book. Unbeknownst to me, I had no idea that Mr. Facebook, was going to help complete the other half of my story!

My God has a personality. In my diary, I have a scripture outlined that says from Amos 3:3: "Can two walk together, except they be agreed?" This was one of the sixteen things I wanted in a man. God did not give me what I wanted; He gave me exactly what I needed. The main two things I wanted on that list were: (1) be converted and (2) love God. Do you know God gave me fifteen out of seventeen things on that list? I can't put my finger on when this happened; however, all I remember is by the third date Mr. Facebook told me to start planning for a wedding. I know God said this man was going to be my husband, and I know he asked my parents if he could day-court me, (Yes I made that up, it is dating and courting in the same context.), but "plan to get married" when he did not even propose yet?

It was different for someone to propose to me without a ring, so this threw me all the way off. During our courting we talked a lot, sometimes all day and sometimes all night. You know how it is when you first date that person and you can't get enough of their conversation? Y'all, I was spitting God and that good food to him, and he was eating it all up.

Somewhere between October and November, he wanted to take a Bible study. He did not have a denomination, but he wanted to learn about the Bible and Adventism. I remember his telling me that if the whole world goes to church on Sunday and is against the Bible's Sabbath, then there must be something to it. Plus, he said when he did go to church on Sunday, he did not like it because it never felt like a true rest day; it felt as if he went to church and then work the very next day. He also highlighted football and how he could watch his games on Sundays and not have to worry about church.

I always say the majority is never right. So I hooked him up with my godfather, who is an elder at one of the churches and also my go-to when I have questions relating to the Bible and life situations. By the second month, he was baptized. After his baptism, I was trying to decide who was going to be a part of the wedding, where we were going to have it, and how I was going to plan such a big event in only ten months.

We came up with the date before he proposed to me. How did we come up with the date? Since we met on October 5th, we wanted to stick with the 5th. We strolled through the calendar and found the first date that landed on a Sunday and was the 5th. Great! We had the date locked down; now I'm pretty much passing time waiting to be engaged and trying to convince my girls that I am getting married and to walk by faith. I mean, this wasn't my first time being engaged. I was engaged four times, twice from the same man. I'm sending him the world's best proposals or anything centered around proposals, hoping he would catch the hint, but little did I know, he knew exactly what he was doing all along.

By now my girls are, like, "Is this really the guy that T is supposed to marry, is T losing her mind or making things up saying that God told her this man was going to marry her? Is she moving too fast? Are we going to waste our money going to a bridal fitting only for things not to flourish?"

I must admit, things were moving super quick, and somewhere in the back of my mind, I was waiting for a way out but at the same time trying to struggle to have faith, and remember this is who God told me was going to be my husband. Have you ever thought you heard God, but you were really talking to yourself in your mind? Some days I would have one of those moments.

It was on a weekday that my cousin and I decided to have a girl's night out. Mind you, I hadn't had a girl's night out with her since I gave up drinking. I talked to Mr. Facebook before I left, and he asked me this dumb question, "Can I have your extra pasta that you get with the "2 for 2" deal?

I nicely responded, "No." Like, why would I give him my favorite pasta, courting or not? I can be very stingy when it comes to the food I love and never gave it any more thought.

He was like, "OK, have a good time."

I'm thinking to myself, How I was going to go out with her without having a cocktail? But we did it and we had a ball! As we were enjoying ourselves at my favorite restaurant, Maggianos, I sent him pictures, like, "I wish you were here." I thought it would be the perfect place for him to propose, but he would never do it.

After dinner, the waiter came out and asked, "Are you ready for dessert?" Then he went on to ask if I drank wine and all of these other irrelevant questions that had nothing to do with my tiramisu.

I responded, "No, I do not drink." I asked the guy, "Sir, can you please bring me my dessert?"

I think I was getting a little irritated because I do not like to eat my food in increments. I like to eat it all together or I lose my appetite. My cousin and I were sitting in the back, a quiet and reserved spot, and across from us was a table of maybe eight Italian people celebrating someone's special occasion. So as I'm observing maybe ten waiters coming out to the table for their special celebration, they weren't going to the table past us. This time they stopped at our table, but what I noticed was that they were escorting someone into the room.

Someone nicely put this big sheet cake in front of me, lit with candles, and it read, Teshawn, I will always love you! Will you marry me?

Then the person slickly said, "You asked for dessert."

I look up, and it is Mr. Facebook saying, "The Bible says, he that findeth a wife findeth a good thing, and I know I found a good thing."

He got down on one knee and pulled out the ring, and asked, "Will you marry me?"

I froze with disbelief. It was almost like I had to rehearse my entire day and how nasty I was to him with the pictures I sent him and talking about him to my cousin saying he would never do anything like this in such a romantic setting. My mouth was open. The table of eight in front of me asked in their accent, "What did she say?"

He was waiting. I was still shocked. I said, "Yes, of course!"

The Italian table said, "She said yes. She said yes. She said yes!"

Mr. Facebook got me good. First, the waiters escorted him in. He was dressed as a waiter, had the cake in his hand, had roses taped to his back, and his mom followed him recording the entire occasion. I was in tenth heaven! I was finally engaged. Wow, I had something to stand on while preparing to get married, and most important, Mr. Facebook did not let me down. He really wanted to get married, so he made it official, and the entire restaurant was in on my surprise. Now, that was America's best proposal!

Trick Challenge

I have a simple yet rewarding challenge. I challenge you to fast and ask God if the person you are dating is really

from God, and if they are not, let go and wait for God
to bring you who He designates to be in your life.

5

FAITH OR
FLUFF?

We were almost finished planning the wedding, everything was etched in stone, and our marriage counseling sessions were complete. The only thing we needed to do was finalize a few things like plan the honeymoon, find a caterer to make the food, and find a makeup artist to take care of my girls' faces. During this time, Mr. Facebook and I were invited to speak at the general conference on how we met through social media and what that experience was like. Well, in the midst of that, I made friends with their makeup artist, who did makeup very well. Somehow, she was so excited about our story that she offered to make up my girls faces for only $10 and mine for $75. We prayed and prayed about everything we were missing in order to finalize our wedding arrangements, after all, the Bible says, "Pray without ceasing" (1 Thessalonians 5:17).One day at work, my mother-in-law called me and asked, "What else do you guys need for the wedding?"

I told her, "A honeymoon!"

It is funny because Mathew 7:7 says, "Ask and it shall be given." Do you know my in-laws paid for us to go to the Cayman Islands?

The final thing we needed was a caterer. My parents ended up paying for it, and that is another story.

Look at how God provided just like that. I was excited about a honeymoon, but then I had questions as to whether or not we should drink wine. After all, we were married, so I prayed and asked God to show me. A few days before our wedding, I went to drop all of my gown and bridal things at my aunt's house because the limo would meet us at her house the day of the wedding.

The moment she met me at the door, she said, "Teshawn, I was in prayer, and the Holy Spirit told me to tell you not to drink on your honeymoon. If you do, you will end up catching "AIDS."

Geesh. Really God, AIDS? You know I am not drinking any more after I heard that. I had to convince myself that this information was coming from a good source, and because she did not know what I asked God to show me, it was my confirmation.

Our wedding was wonderful! There were a few things that

I would do differently if I could redo them, but overall God blessed us and everything was how God wanted it to be. After the wedding was over, our limo driver stuck it out with us until the reception was over at no extra cost. Come to find out, my mom was ministering to him about how she lost a son, and I guess he felt so sad for me that he stayed the entire day, and then asked if we still wanted to take pictures at the harbor.

No sir, we were exhausted. I'm so thankful for him because he made sure we got to our hotel safely, and that was one less thing we had to worry about. That night we were so beat. We chose not to consummate our marriage that night, but rather open our cards and see how much money people gave us, so we could have spending money on our honeymoon. We did not have any money; every bit of money we had, we put toward the wedding. This was our first time officially winging it together. God really was preparing us, whether we knew it or not.

By the way, please do not hold on to the hype. As much as we wanted to get it in, you will be whipped by the end of your marital bliss with no time to think about anything except sleep. The next morning our flight departed at 6 a.m., and off we went to the Grand Cayman Islands. Finally, a getaway, relaxation, and a chance to get it in!

Halfway to arrival the turbulence starts to shake the plane. I and my husband, Mr. Facebook, looked at each other with great concern. What's going on? Then we hear the pilot, "Well, folks, looks like we're landing in a hurricane."

Oh my! The only thing on my mind was, We are about to die and haven't even gotten the chance to get it in, especially because prior to marriage we did not have sex. Oh Lord, help! We're about to die! So then the captain said there was a plane in front of us. "Let's see how they do before we land."

We immediately started praying for, like, ten to fifteen minutes asking God to get us on the ground safely, and soon as we said, "Amen," we heard the captain say he was ready to land the plane. We landed safely, obtained our things, and were waiting for our ride to the Westin Resort! We could not wait to start our honeymoon, and then our taxi driver almost got into a head-on collision with another driver. Satan was really after us, and we hadn't even gotten our feet wet with marriage yet.

When we arrived, they greeted us and had wine and chocolate sent to our room. I kindly asked the front desk, "Can you please send us something other than alcohol? We do not drink." This was hard! Come on; we are in another land, vacation, our honeymoon. It was my husband, for crying out loud. But nope, the Holy Spirit had to remind me of what I prayed about and the consequences. So they sent us ice cream and something to drink other than wine. Our first meal out, trying to budget at the restaurant we said, "Yes, these prices are great, and we have just enough to eat." Only then we found out that it was the queen's money and our money had to be converted. Oh, my. This was a very stressful honeymoon starting off.

We ended up leaving the resort and found a place to eat across the street that served all types of cuisines and we were super happy and satisfied especially coming from me, a chef (in my own mind).

Their food definitely met our standards. Only God directed us to this place, but guess what? We ate twice a day trying to maintain the little money we had to spend. There were times we would eat and think we were in the budget and forgot it wasn't our currency. Shoot! We tried with all our might not to call home to our parents for extra financial support. We were struggling, and nobody ever knew this but us.

To add insult to injury we were there for almost a week. By now we were homesick. Can you believe this? How can you be in paradise and homesick? We tried to go clubbing, but God shut that down because one day I forgot my ID in the hotel, so I automatically knew it wasn't in God's plan. You know God left us with just enough, and then it happened. My husband's payday came around, so we had just enough to sustain us. Praise God until we left!

We finally arrived at the airport to return home and had an extended, eight-hour layover overnight. We did not have money to buy a night at the hotel, so we literally had to lay over. We were trying to kill time by walking around the airport. We had no blankets, it felt like Antarctica. We could not get comfortable, and finally we slept on the cold ground. What a start to the rest of our lives.

This is when we realized no matter how bad it got, we were

in this together. Then I told you, Mr. Facebook, yes he had a job, but it wasn't paying much, but guess what? Right after we got married God gave it all to us. God even gave him a better job making more money. Although Mr. Facebook caught the metro back and forth to work, it was really starting to take a toll on us. The metro was starting to become more dangerous, and his job location ended up changing to another district.

It pays to take up for God. One day we had to figure out how we were going to purchase another car, at the same time we are praying and wearing God's ears out because we did not want to take on any more bills. We prayed for years that God would put us on someone's heart to give us a car. After all, this young lady at our church gave a testimony stating that someone gave her a car, so why couldn't God do the same thing for us?

Well, it just so happened that out of the blue the job wanted him to work during Sabbath hours, and Mr. Facebook had enough faith to say, "Even if I lose my job, I will not work on God's Sabbath."

Moments later we decided to reach out to a family member and ask them about this car that we were about to finance. Mind you, they were well informed about which cars were good to purchase. All of a sudden, the family member said, "I wasn't going to tell you this, but we were planning to take you and Teshawn out to dinner to tell you that we are giving you our car."

Lord Jesus, another testimony for the bank!

We burst out into tears of joy as Mr. Facebook was sitting in front of the subway for the last time. I stand here to say our faith was not fluff. It was real, and for one out of many times, God showed us what happens when you continue to pray and believe, no matter how long it takes for your prayer to be answered.

Two years into our marriage, I found out I was pregnant. I found a new OB because the one I had did not deliver babies. This lady took my blood work and found my HCG levels super high, but she did not know why. I remember my first visit to her. She was mean and nasty and just robotically told me during my checkup she said she could not find a heartbeat and that I miscarried. I wasn't comfortable with her news, so I called my old OB and informed her of what I just heard. She immediately set up a sonogram to see what was going on and why my HCG levels were so high. Well, folks, not only was I pregnant, we found out I was carrying twins. It is funny because I was wondering why the new gynecologist did not know I was carrying twins. I could not tolerate her, so I kicked her to the curb.

After my sonogram, the doctors had this profound look but would not say anything to me at first. The only thing they said was, "I'm sorry." I had no idea what they were talking about until my recent doctor, Dr. Vaughn (RIP), said, "You have a blighted ovum pregnancy."

I think I was in total disbelief at what just took place. I told Mr. Facebook what had happened, and he told me,

"As Christians, we need to handle this situation differently from the world."

I took that with a grain of salt, listened, and we still trusted God. I remember ministering to this church in the southeast that Sunday and singing "Total Praise." I also gave the testimony that I was carrying around this sack with no life, but I trust God, which made me minister to this church even more powerfully. The people were blown away, and the group that I came with texted me, The pastor wanted us to tell you that you will have another baby.

I remember we truly grieved differently. This was the first thing we learned about each other. I'm thinking to myself, "How could he say this to me without consoling me?" It was almost like he sounded bitter—not helpful, just naïve about the entire situation. Then I had to have a dilation and curettage to deal with my miscarriage the day after his birthday, which is a day we will never forget.

I find that men grieve differently from women. My husband was to himself, not affectionate, very quiet, and irritable. It may not go for all men, but my husband says when men are sad, they get angry. When women are sad, we want affection, to be consoled and we need assurance. What I have learned is that true assurance only comes from Jesus Christ.

The day of my D&C we checked into the hospital, and I remember feeling like a zombie, not knowing what to expect with this procedure because I have never had an abortion and this was my first time having a miscarriage.

My husband and I saw two couples in front of us who were pregnant, checking in and about to have their babies, then we heard a bell go off, which meant a baby was born. We had mixed emotions because here somebody's baby was being born, and ours was about to be taken away.

As we were waiting upstairs, my husband silently said, "I'm sorry for how I have been treating you. I'm scared and sad, and I do not want to lose you to this procedure."

I forgave him, we made up, and prayed about the surgery and that God's hand would guide the doctor. As soon as we prayed in came the anesthesiologist, and after she inserted the needle in my hand, she covered the needle to keep it in place with this bandage, then she wrote something on the bandage to inform the doctor, but when I looked down I could read that it said, God sent.

Wow! It was an immediate peace that came over me. It was in that instance that I knew God was going to see us through. Then I fell asleep, and next thing I knew, it was over. I woke up a little drugged but guess what, I was happy to be alive! I knew God was going to look out for us. Three months later, we got pregnant again with our first child together, which was a baby boy.

Trick Challenge

Is there something that God is putting on your heart to do? Did He specifically speak to you and tell you to go somewhere or to remove yourself from something or somebody? I challenge you to obey and reap the reward from your obedience to Him.

6

TRUST AND
OBEY

Soon after we found out I was pregnant, I was in the midst
of a mess at my job. At one point, the entire organization
turned against me due to this one lady's trying to get me
fired because of her own issues about the Sabbath and my
beliefs about working after Sabbath hours on Friday
evening. We all know what it is like to have job troubles,
and I felt I was being persecuted for the sake of God's Sabbath. God ended up telling me through one of my supervisors whom I adored that it was time to look for another
job. Honestly, I do not remember putting my résumé out
there. I just remember the guy writing me a letter of recom-
mendation for my next opportunity.Low and behold, this
company calls out of the blue. They said, "We found you on

Craigslist and wanted to know if you could come in for an interview."

I always promised myself that my next job would not be the same as the last. I was going to do something different. I was going to be more professional, not shoot the breeze with my colleagues, and respect from everyone with my professionalism. I also vowed to get to know the entire 5,000-something employees in the building. Was it for my ego? Maybe, I have always considered myself to be outgoing, so hey, the sky was the limit.

I arrived at the interview confident that I would do what it took to get the job, no matter what and keeping in mind that I was five months pregnant. I was not showing and still had this dilemma of revealing to my potential employer that I was about to have a baby. I was in the interview, praying, "God, please help me." Sometimes that is all it takes when you are in a jam is to call on the name of the Lord.

Most employers will not even look at you when you say you are expecting because they train you for a job only for you to be on maternity leave for three to four months. And trust me, I was taking the full four months.

When I got to the interview, it was a panel of three people in uniforms. I'm waiting for a volley of questions, they only asked me two questions, and of course I had my own set of questions. Then I had to break the moment of honesty to them. I said, "You know how it is when you are selling a house, but the ceiling is cracked with a slight leakage, and only you know the ceiling is cracked with that slight leakage and yet I'm still selling this wreck of a house to you?"

They looked at me confused. I went on to say, "I just wanted to be honest and let you all know I am expecting and wanted to be honest about it." Oh, what relief.

After I said what I thought was a surprise to them, they said, "That is it?"

Oh well, that is wonderful. They were saying I would will do well here because my supervisors and coworkers were all doctors and nurses. "If you want the job is yours."

What an answer once again to prayer, just like that.

The other great news is that because my supervisor knew that I was expecting and soon to go on maternity leave, he said, "I will not fully train you until you get back from leave."

I was, like, what? I'm literally sitting in my cubical getting paid for five months, helping when I can and whenever I can, and it was legal. Some jobs are too good to be true, and I later found out that this was the job that God put us through to test our faith. How sweet was this? I was getting paid almost two grand per month, after taxes. So, to sit back and collect that money was a fantastic experience for me, if I say so myself.

During my pregnancy on this job, the enemy really tried to attack me. One day, I was driving to work in DC, and out of nowhere this numbness started coming over me and taking over my left side. My driving hand started going numb as I was trying to drive; it was awful. I used to suffer from severe back spasms when I was working for the other job due to stress that used to leave me on the floor for hours until the spasm would pass. My evil supervisor at the last job would make me take leave because of this; they would also treat me meanly just because and would not have any mercy on my spasm episodes.

Thinking back, I remember we had severe lightning, flooding, and thunder; this was the type you could see in the trees. Almost like the lightning was hitting the trees and pouring down rain in my area, which was an hour away from my job, and they would not let me call out. There were some times my back would go out, and I would not be able to go to work for three days. That was very stressful back then because I was a single parent. I had bills to pay, and I had a daughter to take care of with no help.

Fast-forward, this time was the worst out of all the times. I arrived at my job just in time, only for the doctors and nurses to call 911. Everyone thought I was having a stroke and was scared for the baby. Mr. Facebook's nerves were shot. He was trying to figure out who could take care of our daughter and who would go with me in the ambulance because he could not get to me at that time. Guess what? Jesus went with me the whole ride to the hospital.

I arrived at the first hospital, and some close church members of ours came to pray over me. Then they had to transfer me to another hospital for more testing. I had never gone through anything like it. I knew it was warfare, but I knew whatever I was going through wasn't too hard for God. Meanwhile, I was praying the entire time, like, "Lord, please fix this situation. Block the enemy and cover me with your blood. I do not know what to expect, but I know you are in control."

A few hours after being admitted, we get the results back, and thankfully, I wasn't stroking out. I was diagnosed with anxiety, but I rejected that.

Wow, halfway through my maternity leave, here came another trial. Although we prayed my entire four months of maternity leave and needed to find a daycare provider within this time frame, I had to inform my boss I wasn't coming back until I found someone. We were having a hard time with finding someone decent, and can you believe this man had me on maternity leave for nine months? (I did not take it all.) Unbelievable! This supervisor was the best supervisor I had ever worked for in all my working years. He appreciated my assistance so much; he was willing to extend my maternity leave until I found the right provider. Ladies and gents, I call this a favor.

For four months we were searching for that perfect daycare provider in our area, and not one person was worthy or met our expectations. We were looking for a provider who would not stick our child in front of the television all day, who was fair but a stern disciplinarian, who would do right by our son, who would teach him character, and most important, who lived nearby. That Saturday before I had to return to work, we decided to attend a church down the street from our house, and it wasn't until I ran into one of my good friends, Renee, that God answered our prayers. It was so divine. Out of nowhere I get this tap on my shoulder, I turned around and here's the question, "How are you, gal?"

I said, "Searching for a perfect provider for my son, so I can return back to work by Monday."

In that moment she says, "Do not worry, girl. God has it. I have the perfect person for you!"

I could not believe that. Could it be that God was finally answering our prayer after four months, and was He really going to come through for us? She went on to say, "The lady I know lives not too far from here, she doesn't watch TV and is very hands-on with the children in her center—bingo! I was sold and had never met the lady. She gave us the number; we met Mrs. Fran the very next day, and we both had a feeling of assurance that this was the place God wanted our son to be. Her place was immaculate, very cozy, nice arrangement, a back yard, a few kids, comfortable, but most important, she loved the Lord! She was everything my friend from church said she was and more.

Our son attended her daycare that Monday, and what a happy young lady I was going back to work. I was on top of the world.

Not even a month into returning back to work another trial hit us. My landlord informed me that we needed to start looking for somewhere else to live because she was selling our building. Let's be clear, my husband and I were paying around $800 a month for a two-bedroom, two-bath spot near the DC metro stop down the street, stores down the street, everything convenient in a nice neighborhood, and oh boy, here was another dilemma. I honestly did not know where we were supposed to go, but God did. We had faith, right?

It's funny because when I was single I tried for at least seven years to buy a house on my own, and nothing would work. God shut everything down. I had contracts on a few houses, and they fell through. I remember this one condo I had a contract on and was going to purchase, and guess what? They ended up on the news the next day because of the landlord doing some cruddy things. So, at least I knew if God were with me then and had my back, I knew He had it now, especially being that I was married and we were trying to do the right things. Not only did we need to find housing, but say I wanted to quit my job to come back home and take care of my own son. I wouldn't be able to because now we had to use my income so I could help buy the house.

One day I decided to do my husband a favor and go pick my stepson up. I knew he was tired and did not want to drive over an hour away when he got off from work, so why not? Right before I got to my stepson's house, I hit the corner and saw this housing sign in plain sight that says, We pay for closing costs. I called Mr. Facebook and said, "You would not believe what just happened. I saw a brand new house sign for sale, and the billboard said they pay for closing costs."

What? I know God sent me to pick this boy up because if I did not go out of my way, we would have missed our blessing. We reached out to them, and the next thing we knew, we were starting the process to be first-time homeowners.

OK, then it hit us. Our next dilemma was coming up with $13,000 in three months, and I had just returned from maternity leave. I do not know about my husband, but I know I was nervous about this because now the pressure was on.

I kind of doubted my husband's capabilities. I figured, how could he take care of this when he's never lived on his own and never really took care of a big task like this? Come on, these are my thoughts. I was scared, and it was a part of my lack of faith at that moment. The Holy Spirit had to remind me that "what God has for me is for me and He makes no mistakes" (Genesis 18:14). I honestly did not think God knew my husband could handle this task.

You do not think God knew that my husband could handle this? My scripture of comfort during that moment was, "Be strong and of a good courage, fear not, nor be afraid of them: for the Lord thy God, he is that doth go with thee; he will not fail thee, nor forsake thee" (Deuteronomy 31:6).

I can't tell you how we came up with this money, but rest assured, nobody gave it to us. Even when the pain-in-the-behind finance people wanted me to give them, in detail, where the money was coming from, I could not put it down on paper. To this day, I just know that money started coming from all different directions, and it was only God. I do remember getting $2,500 that I can confidently jot down that came in from Aflac due to my labor and delivery, but that is all I can jot down on paper.

God supernaturally helped us come up with that money. We serve a good God. God knows what we need and what we want. My go-to scripture of promise was always, "Delight thyself also in the Lord: and he shall give thee the desires of thine heart" (Psalms 37:4), and He did just that. I have always wanted to live in a three-level brick-front townhouse, and one day my husband said to me, "If that is the house you want, that is the house you will get because you deserve it."

Not only did we end up buying this house, but we were able to go into the warehouse and personally handpick every detail of this God-given blessing, and isn't this something that it wasn't until I got married that God allowed us to make this move together? We went to closing, relocated, and everything went super smooth. God made it a great transition.

I always loved my job. The joy about this contract was that we were allowed to take two fifteen-minute breaks and an hour lunch break. I went outside almost every day. One thing about me from childhood that I still cling to is that I love the outdoors, and I must take my walks. By the way, my boss and my contract were two separate entities. I had the best boss because he resided in another location, he did not micromanage me, and I worked better that way, but my main company was different.

After moving to our new house and finding another day-care that was located on the same street as our house, the employees there started making me feel very insecure about our son in their possession. After my walks for lunch, I would contemplate the day I could quit to stay home and take care of my own son. I enjoyed being outside and not being on anyone's time. I had always admired my one cousin who did not work at the time. She was always avail-able to help others. I wanted to be available to help others and be on my own schedule. I never thought of calling my husband and asking him if I could quit because on my prior job, I tried it before I had my son, and he said, "No, we have bills." And this was before we purchased the house, so you know he wasn't having that.

Since I could not quit, there were days I would pop up at various hours just to peek in and see how they were treat-ing my beloved treasure, and every time I did, his nose was always running and his diaper would always need to be changed or have poop piled up in it. At this point, I'm on fire at the way our son is being treated. I started missing our son, especially being at work pumping. Nursing at the time was torment. It was another full-time job. Every three hours my boss would let me go upstairs and pump for my son to eat.

Let's not forget, I felt very comfortable with Mrs. Fran, and

I did not trust this new daycare center. My spirit started grieving the fact that he was placed in this jailhouse of a center. After we left Mrs. Fran's daycare and transitioned him to this new one, I would call every day to speak to him and although he could not talk, I would ask him how they were treating him. They would comment, "Aw, that is nice that you are speaking to him like he's an adult."

"Um, excuse me, miss, he's a human."

See, that comment right there can show you how badly these people would grind my gears. Thinking back, I didn't notice that a child would be there for a week and then turn up missing. Some would be there for a few days and never return. I would wonder what it was all about, but no one would let me know what was going on until things started happening to my son.

I will never forget the program we attended at Restoration Praise Center. They had a guest speaker who came to tell us about his story. He briefly described how God moved him to quit his job and how he had to tell his wife. That is the only thing I heard, his testimony of leaving the job and his faith. Everything else is pretty much a blur.

I gently nudged my hubby, like, "Did you hear that?" I can't pinpoint it, but within that week I found the speaker on Facebook and in-boxed him on Facebook Messenger. I told him I was thinking about leaving my job as well but wasn't sure how to do it. That man said one thing that changed my whole world. He said, "Sis, in order to walk on water, you must be able to step out of the boat."

When he said this, I thought hard on that response for, like, a good week. I could not shake that response. On my way to the organic market near our house, I called my husband to tell him what the speaker said to me. Standing outside in the cold, pacing back and forth, discussing this situation with my husband: it was that moment that we verbalized we did not have faith.

I mean, come on. Faith? We all have some form of faith if you think about it. Well, what happens when God puts you on the hot seat to force your hand to see what you are really made of? Within that week, around December, the Holy Spirit impressed me to speak to my boss. How ironic, he was in town that week out of all the weeks. I quietly snuck into his cubical and started quietly talking.

"Boss, for some reason, I do not think I'm going to be here too much longer." Did I just say that? This was the best job I have ever had, making almost $60,000, and this was my end result. I went on to say, "One day, the market will crash and our dollar will no longer be of any value, and I do not want to just start having faith in God when that happens. I would rather start now?" What? Now I'm talking to my boss about God and politics?

My boss gently said, "Teshawn, when you do plan to leave, all I ask is that you give me ninety days."

Ninety Days? Um, I'm not even sure if I'm leaving; I'm just putting the bug in your ear just in case, but OK.

Here comes another trial. At this point, my son is being

physically abused in this daycare and nobody can seem to tell me what happened or who did it. One day we pick him up and he has bite marks on his nose. Another day we pick him up and he has scratch marks on his face. For those of you who love your kids and know how much I love mine, this type of thing can make you jump in your flesh. I could have, but I'm not sure why I did not. I am positive Jesus dispatched all His heavenly angels to come down and rescue me from jumping back in the trick bag of bondage by—OK, moving forward!

Two months later, here comes my next trial. On my way to work on this certain wonderful highway, which was backed up with traffic from here to eternity, I get this phone call from my favorite older cousin Harriet. Some of us can appreciate a good conversation while in traffic; however, this was not the particular conversation that this working-woman wanted to hear. As we were talking, here comes the moment of truth: "Teshawn when are you going to leave your job to come home and get your house in order?"

What? Leave my job? My house is in order. This particular question kind of threw me for a loop. My response was, "I'm not. Matter a fact, after I pay off my credit and debit cards and student loans, then I will leave my job."

The Holy Spirit quickly took over her and instead of my cousin's voice speaking, it is almost like God placed Himself in her and started speaking to me. The voice said, "That is not how God works. God waits for you to make the move first, and He will do the rest." Then that same voice said, "If you do not leave your job, I will put you in a position where you will be forced to leave."

Oh my! I know that wasn't my cousin who spoke those words. I immediately knew it was God who told me to leave. Her voice came back on the line. I started thinking quickly, You are going to put me in a position to leave my job if I do not leave on my own? What will happen to me? Will my son die in daycare messing with these trifling people? Oh Lord.

With urgency, I told my cousin, "We have to pray. I have to go to work and call my husband and tell him God told me to leave my job." Will he believe me? Will he think I have ulterior motives? I did not want to leave. I made good money. I like people. Plus, my grandma was a stay-at-home mom. But I knew I had to bite the bullet and inform my boss.

First things first, I needed to tell my husband.

I got to work with a sense of urgency. This particular morning, I needed to go upstairs to my room I usually pump in. There was privacy, I could pray, and then I could tell my husband what God said. I called my hubby up and before I said a word, I quoted, "But without faith it is impossible to please him: for he that cometh to God must believe that he is, and that he is a rewarder of them that diligently seek him" (Hebrews 11:6). Then I told him the conversation I had with my cousin about how God spoke through her and told me to leave my job. I got silent and waited to hear what he had to say.

He responded, "I know this is God."

I know this is God? We just purchased this new house, the mortgage was high, and we thought we were struggling with the money we were making together. He agreed that God wanted me to leave this wonderful job, only to come home and struggle? We discussed it, and with the big faith he had, he said, "I know, this is what God wants, even if we lose our house."

When I brought this situation to my husband, it was almost like I needed to hear this reassurance from him, negating the straight command from God, and yet again, at that moment, I was broken all the way down yet again.

It seemed like history was repeating itself. Remember when the pastor told me he was going to be my husband? Three years later, I was repeating the very same scenario but a different situation. Wow! That same day, after my hubby was convinced that God told me to leave, I submitted my resignation to my supervisor.

My boss knew that day was coming, he just did not know when. During my ninety days of preparing to leave, I finally understood why God gave me ninety days to retire. He wanted me to reach all 5,000 of the people in that building, and if not all, close to it. I tried to keep my retiring on a low, but everyone found out, and when they did the questions started coming in. "Teshawn, didn't you guys just buy a house? Are you going to be able to afford it? Are you really leaving this job to work on your company?"

By the way, I had a vegetarian catering company at the time, and most of my clients were located in my building. Almost everyone thought I was leaving my job to work for myself full-time. My response, "No, I'm not leaving to start my company. It takes money to make money."

God told me to leave to get my house in order. If God told me to leave, then that means He will take care of us. I was tired of explaining myself. Plus, I was nervous because I had two darn incomes from my paycheck and my side hustles from people patronizing my company at work.

When I look back, I'm glad God wanted me to make that move. My home was a wreck, and we were hit or miss. My hubby held the house down in the morning; I held it down in the evening when he left to go to work. I did not have time to focus on our daughter. We never spent any time together because we were all over the place with everything. So, having God tell me to leave was a good thing. God knows, I will never forget this day. As I was leaving the café with my back turned, this big-shot boss confronts me in front of everyone. He demanded, "So, what are you going to do when you go home, go back to school and get a degree? How are you supposed to afford that?"

Why was this man questioning God, let alone my plans for my life? Excuse me, sir, you do not know me in the first place. My face turned red for his even questioning what God is capable of. One thing I do not like is when people question God and how big He is, but most important, what He can do for His children who love him and want to please Him. I will admit although I did not truly have faith, it wasn't until that moment the little faith I did have nicely rose up on that certain boss.

I firmly and happily responded in front of everyone as my back was still facing him. I turned around and said, "The same God that told me to go home and get my house in order is that same God that will take care of us, and further-more, I already have a degree." Then I turned back around and walked away. The man's face turned red, but guess what? Do not come for my Father, God.

A lot of us do not realize how much power God has. Plus, to be brutally honest, He doesn't need us to defend Him. Do you really think God would tell me to leave my great-pay-ing job and not take care of me? The last week on my job, something happened that I always wanted.

My job had something super special for me. The supervisor and some of my team wanted to take me and whomever I invited out to eat. I chose my favorite spot, which was across the street. This place was expensive, but this café sold a black bean tofu that I can still taste as I type. I invited my husband, and they treated him as well.

When my small gathering was over, we returned to the job, and the colleagues from the contract we worked for had stayed behind to help surprise me with this super sweet set up in the conference room. I wish I could show you the pic-ture. It was a cupcake theme. Then they went on to present me with a pink chef's apron with monogrammed initials. For once, I was leaving a job and they acknowledged my work ethic. They actually appreciated my contribution. At all the other jobs they would try to terminate me, and when I did put my resignation in, it would not be a sincere going-away party, and I did not want to sit around a bunch of fake people and eat. It was almost like Jesus' Last Supper and breaking bread with Judas. No, thank you. That wasn't my cup of tea.

I tell you when God gives you a going-away party, God does it up. He gave me a cute, posh going-away party with all the things I liked. He allowed the planning committee to dig deep into what they were going to do for me. To name a few things that I can remember, they served fruit, cupcakes, drinks, chips, and cookies. My entire floor came, and some of the people that I was friends in the building were there. I have never been so honored to leave a job on such good terms in all my life. Our God does it up for those who love Him and do not ever forget that.

Here was my last confirmation prior to leaving my job of how I knew God was going to come through for us. My last day at my job, I wanted to host a luncheon because our cafeteria did not know how to cater to the vegetarians in the building. So, I wanted to provide a luncheon with three of my top vegetarian entrees, along with some sides and desserts, to show these people what vegetarian food really tastes like. I wanted to make my mark here and not only be known for my personality, but also for my food.

Prior to getting things in order, I always ask God, "If you want me to do something, work things out; if not, shut them down." I spoke to one of the directors at my job to discuss my plans for my last day before I retire and they thought this was a great idea. Someone connected me to the building's custodian manager; this was the main person I had to speak to to set up a small area in the cafeteria's dining room. I sent an email, and the person raved about how much they thought this was a great idea. Then they gave me a parking pass to park in the garage beneath us with the big wigs, so I could unload my food and décor.

Isn't God good? I was happy to know that God approved of my idea. I sent an email to invite the director of the entire building, her executives, and all the main supervisors in the building. By the way, the company was and still is to this day a big deal, so for me to send an email and obtain a response was a blessing. My last day arrives. I cooked the night before to lay out this big spread of yummy food to show these people how real vegetarians eat, and God performed a miracle. Although the director could not attend, she sent some fruit platters and veggie platters to contribute to my meal, and that was the first time that I saw my two fish and five loaves being stretched. Listen, I made food for fifty to a hundred people, and that food almost fed the whole building. People kept coming and coming and coming. I would check the pans to see if the food were gone and not see anything in those pans, but the people kept on eating. The luncheon was successful, and I greeted my guests to say farewell. Right before I exited the building, as I'm packing my last belongings, the group that I supported wanted me to come see them one more time. They wanted to take our last picture together. All of a sudden, they handed me an envelope.

They said, "Teshawn, We know you funded this entire luncheon out of your pocket, and we are very thankful. In honor of you giving back, we went around the building and took up a collection to give some of the money back to you, to help offset the cost for lunch."

Unbelievable! That was the moment that I knew God was going to take our faith to another level. The day I left my high-paying job to do what my Father asked me to do was the day that He truly took care of all our needs. "Behold, to obey is better than sacrifice" (1 Samuel 15:22). I stand here today to say that walking on water has never seemed so easy and our lives have never been the same.

Trick Challenge

Some of you may have set some high standards for your potential mate, and although this seems nice, I challenge you to court the next person that you know God sent you. How do you know He sent them? A true man or woman of God will:

- Bring God to the table.

- Ask your parents to court you.

- Not try to control you.

- Not ask to sneak preview your cheeks.

- Not want to live with you before marriage.

- Wait to have sex.

- Not put you in a position or mindset to give up yourself in any way.

- Date your mind.

- Add to and not subtract from you.

- Be willing to group date you.

7

POWER OF SUBMISSION

Since stepping out on faith, we have been tested on every end, and I mean every end, but God has not failed us. God has come through for us every time. When I first came home, I struggled with having the faith that the bills would get paid. So, the first two years of my coming home to get the house in order was based on my trusting God. Although my hubby said he did not have faith, he really did, so this trial of my coming home was truly for me. He had faith from the very beginning. Every month, when the mortgage was due, my family would find me smack-dab in the middle of our kitchen floor crying and praying for God to move on our behalf, to bless us to be able to pay it. I mean, we just got the house, and in my mind I really wanted to enjoy it and not get kicked out on the streets because God asked me to come home and sacrifice everything. You all, it got so bad it was like clockwork, every month for two years the same old stuff. If I had known then what I know now, things would be totally different.

My daughter would say out loud to my husband, "Why is Mommy crying?" Oh, the mortgage must be due!

I'm not going to lie; there were times we did not have enough money to eat, and still we do not at times. But right in the nick of time, almost at the last moment, God would come through for us, and He's still doing it to this day. I think we get things twisted. Philippians 4:19 says, "But my God shall supply all your need according to his riches in glory by Christ Jesus," and this is exactly what He means. As time went by, He started using other people to bless us. One day we were in need of some money to pay a few bills and buy some food, and all of a sudden, this random lady was trying to reach out to me through a family member and said, "God told me to put some money in your bank." I was, like, what? OK. I gave the lady my bank information, checked the account, and there it was: $500. What? $500.

Now saints, you know and I know to give away $500 just like that is rare, so you know God had to impress it upon this lady's heart. The crazy thing is that these unusual situations started happening all the time. Until one day I finally got it, and when I got it, guess what happened? God allowed me to have more kids because I finally came to the point that God would not bring me this far to leave me as the homemaker and running the house. He had to start with me first. Isn't that something?

After that I finally got the message that God wasn't going to leave me in the dark, but instead elevate me. Here we go again. I went grocery shopping one Saturday night, and out of nowhere as I'm putting away the groceries, my wooden serving tray jumps out from beside my refrigerator and—boom—breaks my toe. Now I can't drive and have to rely on God, yet again, to get me and my two kids from point A to point B. Then as I was bored in the house, relying on others to take me from point A to point B, I started having these weird cravings. I thought to myself, "Let me get a random test just to see what's going on and—boom—it hit me like a ton of bricks—I tested positive. OK, God!

Let me say this, God will never give us more than what we can handle, even if at times, you can't seem to control a fly. Ever since I started having kids, I know it was God's doing, and guess what else? If God allows you to have kids, please know He will take care of them too. Since having kids, I have never had to buy clothes, shoes, or main essentials. God will use anyone to take care of His kids. Every time they go to the next size, guess what? Someone will call out the blue and say, "I have clothes for you," or whatever we need they will have.

Let's get something straight, I was relying on God for almost everything, but I was bored in the house. I gave my life to God and got baptized prior to meeting my husband. I gave up drinking and never went back, gave up porn, gave up all these various things that I did in my past. Please do not think the devil will not come to tempt you all over again. He will put things back in your path that you thought you overcame. He's a persistent and relentless ancient demon who has been studying the human race for thousands of years. The great thing about God is that God allows Satan to test us as well as to see where we are and who is who.

Let me make this clear. You can be as busy as you want, but the trick bag still exists. Out of nowhere (remember, I'm just a few years into my marriage), a few kids in, and wham, back into porn. You may ask yourself. If God has been doing all these great things in my life, why would I go back to the trick bag? That is a great question. You know what happened? An idle mind is the devil's workshop. Not trying to play the blame game, but things started getting really busy in my household. My husband became a fire-fighter, and during our time apart I have no idea how I got myself into that bag of lust all over again. What I can say is that curiosity killed the cat. That is what happened.

While on social media, my mind came across one bad thought, and it was like I became this porn fiend all over again. It was horrible. Even in my pregnancy I was, like, Lord, please do what you need to do to deliver me from this spirit. Then the devil started making me feel the feeling of being broken all over again. Remember, I told you demons are relentless. Sometimes you just have to fight with fasting and praying. Isn't it something that you could be silently fighting with these types of demons all by yourself? You are a slave held captive in your own mind because you are too scared to reach out for help. I mean, sometimes anything will do. Just to have someone pray for you is enough.

That is how I got through my last round of porn tricks. I prayed so hard. I admitted to God, I did not want to go back to being the person I used to be. I did not want my unborn child to struggle with what I was consuming. If you could only imagine my feelings and thoughts during this time, hormones raging, emotions out of whack, the old man trying to rise back up in me, but what got me through was the fact that I had a few prayer partners praying for me. I did not tell them what they were praying about, I just said, "Please, pray for me."

Oh, if you could just touch the hem of Jesus' garment, you will be made whole. I can only imagine what the woman with the issue of blood felt like. To have the type of sickness that she had for all of those years, but one day, she came across Jesus and touched His garment and she believed. That is the whole key to overcoming, to believe and to have enough faith for yourself that God will heal whatever your disease is. Your disease could be gambling, drinking, cursing, being negative, gossiping, being nosey, sexing, porn, stripping, hustling, popping pills, drugs, and so on. I want to encourage you to reach out and touch the hem of God's garment, and He will make you whole.

Sometimes you got to run from the trick; do not put yourself in your old environment or you will fall. 1 Corinthians 15:33: "Be not deceived: evil communications corrupt good manners [morals]." I want to encourage you today that victory is coming and that we serve an on-time God. God knows where your heart is, He knows your desires just like He knew my heart. He knows when you are truly sorrowful like David after David committed adultery with another man's wife and then had the nerve to get that man killed. He finally came to grips with God and asked God in Psalms 51:10 to "Create in him a clean heart and I could feel his passion as he said, oh God, (hitting his chest on his knees), and renew a right spirit within me."

I can imagine how David felt to be renewed. When I learned to replace the things I was watching with wholesome things, that is when I got different results. Then I started understanding the straightforward scripture in Philippians 4:8: "Finally, brethren, whatsoever things are true, whatsoever things are honest, whatsoever things are just, whatsoever things are pure, whatsoever things are lovely, whatsoever things are of good report, if there be any virtue, and if there be any praise, think on these things."

I know you heard the saying, to get different results, you have to do something different? I put this to practice, and it worked. It was only when I got off of social media that my load got lighter, my struggles evaporated, and I started focusing on the promise and not the problem.

My mom's favorite saying to me is, "If you have the faith, God's got the power." Well, I'm passing this on to you today, to say if you have the faith, God's got the power, and as you learn to lean on God to have your back in everything, your load will start feeling a lot lighter. Even if it is your thought process or worry about how things will be taken care of like my money issues.

Money has always been a test for me. I have always been put through situations where money was involved. It could be anything from an innocent doctor's bill to every appliance in my new house breaking down. I do not know about you, but money used to serve as a safeguard. You need money to do everything. How did I overcome the trick bag of money? It all happened when I was on my way to deliver some food to one of my clients. My car needed an oil change and gas that day, and we were down to our last $2 in the bank. I'm sure you are asking, "Do people really have $2 left in the bank?"

Well, if you are living on a single income, it happens sometimes, but as long as you return your tithe and offerings you will be fine. Give God His first, and He will take care of the rest. After I put the last coins in my tank, my car started acting up. I would drive on backroads and it would randomly cut off on me.

I was on my way to my client on the beltway and struggling to get there, and what happens but the car cuts off. I'm hot at this moment because my car only had 135,000 miles and it's acting up. I dropped the food off to my client and prayed the entire way down the road hoping to make it to my mechanic before they closed. I pull up and the man gives me a consultation that says your transmission is gone and then gives me a fee of $25.

I immediately burst into tears. My transmission is gone and I need to give you $25? I had no money on me. I felt like an abandoned child because my husband could not leave work to help me, and I had mixed emotions because my brother died in a car accident. Then I wasn't feeling like my family was coming through for me and couldn't care less if anything happened to me. I just got my last oil change and put a fresh tank of gas in the car with the last bit of money in our account. Isn't that a reason to burst into tears?

I can remember the mechanic at the shop saying, "Do not worry about the fee, Mrs. Logan. It is all right." Then he handed me a paper towel.

I said, "I'm not crying about my test. I'm crying because of my day." I honestly did not want God to feel like I was cracking under pressure with this weighty test He gave me. I just had a really bad day.

Then I thought, here we go, back to relying on others for transportation. Later that day, I caught a ride from one of my cousins that I was scared to ride with, but God had to test my faith indefinitely this time. I felt He was testing me to the max. I frantically hitched a ride to my grandma's house that same day, and prior to getting in her car, I remember saying, "God, I trust you" and right after that, my fear of riding with her disappeared and never returned.

The next day, my son wanted to walk down the block to the park, but I told him after he took his nap we would go to the park. This boy took the shortest nap on earth, like, thirty minutes, and was so anxious to go. I did not get upset that his nap was that short because it was warm out that day. We left out to go to the park, my daughter had to bum a ride with someone after school because this is now sports season and here God goes sitting me down yet again. I'm thinking silently, What does God want me to learn now? It seems like every time He sits me down it's because I need to learn something.

The daughter came to meet us at the park, and as we started walking back home, she said, "Mom, I sure would like to have some grapes."

I told her to ask God. I just spent our last money on this car, only for it to die. I said we did not have any money. I felt bad; we did not even have $5 to get the girl some grapes. Well, somehow, I ended up on the phone with my mom and as we start walking on my street, I look to my left and found $20 on top of the grass. I was, like, "Mom, I just found $20." Then I walked a little further and found $20 more dollars. I was, like, "Mom, I just found $20 more." We walked a little further and found a $50. I was, like, "Mom, I just found $50.

My mom was, like, "Girl, bye," and hung up. I guess it was too much excitement.

My daughter went over to the grass and said, "Let me see what I can find. She found nothing but I went back over in the same spot to make sure I did not overlook anything else and another $20 appeared. Just like that, I knew that God put that money over in that grass. Why do you think I said that? The money was wet, and the grass was dry! I immediately kneeled in the streets and praised God for turning our

$2 bank account into $112 just like that, and guess what? After that day, I never had a problem trusting God with money again.

I needed to work on the surrender aspect. I ended up selling my car to CarMax for only $300, but I needed the money, so I gave it up. During my downtime and the process of trusting God for transportation, my husband and I found out I was pregnant again. So, now we have one car, three children and one on the way, so we started looking for trucks! We got this bright idea that we needed a big boy, but nothing would come through for us.

At one point my dad said we needed to get a van. A van? No thanks.

My response was, "I'm not a soccer mom." We got into it with this van ordeal and my thoughts were, What if you wanted a Corvette but someone wanted you to get a Pinto? How would you feel? I tell you everyone we came in contact with seemed to start suggesting this van shenanigan. We were, like, "Cut the comedy; we're not getting no stupid van."

Funny part is, one day a good girlfriend and her husband came over to pick this cake up I had made for her birthday. We looked outside, and what did they have? A van! It did not look like a van; it was nice. Right after they came over, my other dad came over to check out some work that needed to be done. I wasn't home, but he suggested to the hubby, "You all should get a van, and your life will never be the same."

The very next day, one of my catering friends called me out the blue to talk. I told her everything I was going through within the past months. I said, "My car just died on me, and I just found out we are expecting again."

My friend immediately said, "Girl, you need a van. It will not only be good for your kids but for your catering company as well."

Then right after she said that, the very next day, I said to my hubby, "Maybe we should get a van." That day our prayer changed and instead of "God, we need a truck," it was "God, we want what you want for us," and two days later, you guessed it! We got a van.

Weeks into my pregnancy I started off with the wrong craving. Here we go again. Remember how Hennessey and Coca-Cola was my favorite drink? Well, I never dropped the habit of drinking the soda because when I drank it, it reminded me of how I used to drink the alcohol. Meanwhile, the craving for Coca-Cola hit me like a baseball bat, and once again there I was, pregnant with my leg halfway in and halfway out the trick bag. A few things out of many that I learned about how longsuffering my Father is includes that God will put you through the same tests until you truly learn to overcome. Like an umbilical cord, the spirit that was attached to something in my trick bag which was the Coca-Cola, which carried an association with alcohol. This is what created an invisible umbilical cord the enemy still had access to, which in turn left an open door the devil used to influence me. Unbeknownst to me, God was bringing me deliverance in that area. I realized as I got the test that the power of the thing that once had me bound was broken. Let's call this a domino effect in my life. That is why he constantly repeats in the book of Revelations to overcome.

How did I overcome the coke? I'm glad you asked. Seems like everyone in my family knew my struggle was this ridiculous drink. My son would harass me every time I went to McDonald's to buy it: "Mom, the baby doesn't need that drink." And then I could feel my husband staring at me whenever we would go out to dinner and I would buy it. My mother would call to pray and start praying about this caffeine.

It was horrible. I wanted everyone to stop sweating me about this stupid drink, like, what's so bad about it anyway? I mean, I could almost hear this little voice speak to me and say, what's so bad about sin or I would think of how Eve went through the motions of eating that fruit. Honestly, I saw a documentary about soda and its effects. The sugar, acid, and caramel coloring are not good for our bodies at all.

I heard a sermon, and the man of God said, "If you keep abusing your body with the wrong things, you may not pay now but you will pay." Have you ever heard, "payday someday"? OK. Yes, I heard all of these things and I knew better, but guess what I started doing? I started hiding my sweet addiction to this tasty beverage.

See, when I used to drink, I would also drive with the Henny and Coke in the coke bottle; it was my riding buddy.

So, this time around minus the alcohol, I was used to riding around with the coke. One day I even picked a fight with my hubby because I did not want him to know I was going to buy some coffee. It is, like, this caffeine thing was tag-teaming me. If I weren't drinking one, I was drinking the other. I wanted to go spend some time with my mother-in-law, but during my drive I wanted to stop and get me some coffee. This spot had assorted creamers, assorted sugars, and assorted coffee, if you could only imagine the entice-ment. So I wanted to drink that on my way to see her. Then my hubby wanted to blow it by coming with me. I got mad because I did not want him to know I was still drinking this crap. I was supposed to be free, right? The next day we were on our way to our daughter's basketball game, and prior to the game we made a stop at the store. What did I do? Pur-chased the soda and hid it in my coat.

We arrived at the game, and I was making excuses to go out into my van only to consume this beverage. By this time I had enough, I was burnt out from trying to hide what I was doing. I was tired of going back and forth with this one lit-tle stupid but addictive beverage.

So, what happened? I was invited to a night of prayer at this church down the street. I was a little late, but when I walked in the sanctuary, the person leading out started talking about bondage and addictions. For the exercise they asked us to get into small groups to pray about what we were going through. I was never so excited to pray about that addiction. I shared with the two people how it was dri-ving me crazy and how I needed deliverance. Guys, after we prayed that prayer, God gave me freedom from that drink, and this, my friends, was the last eye-opener that God had to show me to fully surrender and be submissive of the power that He offers and the peace that surpasses all understanding; if only I had surrendered earlier.

Throughout my many trials, I have learned that God wants us to trust Him and take Him at His word. I also would like to mention that no matter how big or small your bondage may be, God understands. I know some of you may say what about soda? Or it could be something as petty as ice. Your bondage is your bondage, so when the naysayers talk about your bondage and make it seem like it is nothing, that doesn't mean it is nothing to God.

We serve an intimate Father. God cares, and He will pull you through it. I have plenty of testimonies such as the one I just shared. However, I want to encourage you that if God can free my mind from various bondages, the near-rise of my old personality, the love of money, and worrying about how God was going to take care of us, then I want to say God can do anything for you. God wants to free us from the trick bag; He wants to deliver us from ourselves. We are our own worst enemies. There will be days when you will feel like a failure. There will be days when you will fall down, but do not worry; just get back up again and start over. 1 John 1:9 says, "If we confess our sins, he is faithful and just to forgive us our sins, and to cleanse us from all unrighteousness." God can't lie, so as you acknowledge your sin and repent, He is faithful to cleanse you from all unrighteousness. The goal is to be an overcomer of all sin.

God reiterates all throughout Revelations that to endure is to overcome, so give it a shot and God will be right there to carry you through!

I declare and decree power and victory over your lives. I speak the Spirit of being more than a conqueror over you. Always remember and do not ever forget God is a good God. He's a great God. He can do anything but fail. He has moved so many mountains out of my way. My God is a wonderful God! Psalms 34:8 says, "O taste and see that the Lord is good: blessed is the man that trusteth in him." Psalm 136:1 says, "O give thanks unto the Lord; for he is good: for his mercy endureth forever!" May you learn to trust in God, lean on Him moment by moment, and the power of submission will become easy.

———————

Trick Challenge

Find someone to pray for you that you know can get a prayer through. Out of all of my struggles and addictions, I always had someone to pray me through, but I did a lot of praying as well. I challenge you to learn how to pray and talk to God about everything, so instead of depending on someone else to pray for you, you will know how to get a prayer through.

FINAL THOUGHTS

Commit this to memory:

Sincere

Intimate

Personal

Without a SIP relationship with Jesus, you will die from spiritual dehydration. Take a SIP in the morning, a SIP in the evening, and another SIP at night; and I promise that your spiritual well will **never** run dry.

"But whosoever drinketh of the water that I shall give him shall never thirst; but the water that I shall give him shall be in him a well of water springing up into everlasting life." (John 4:14).

CONTACT THE AUTHOR

Teshawn Logan:

freedomfromthetrickbag@gmail.com

When you write, please include your testimonial or tell me how this book helped you in any way. I'd love to hear from you.

To Purchase Additional Books:

www.amazon.com

Also Available on all Popular ebook Apps

ABOUT THE AUTHOR

Teshawn Logan is from Charles County, Maryland. She is a serial entrepreneur whose heart is built to serve and please God in every area of her life. She enjoys helping those in need and showing her family, church family, and community another way to eat healthy through her healthy Vegetarian and Vegan Cuisines Company, which enhances the knowledge and lifestyle of a whole foods diet. Teshawn is a mom of 5 children, singer, songwriter, author, clothing designer, and a contributing writer for a vegan lifestyle column.